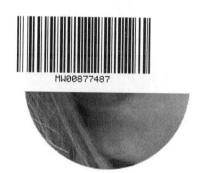

LEARN ARMENIAN IN 52 WEEKS

LEARN ARMENIAN IN 52 WEEKS
WITH 7 SENTENCES A DAY

In the same collection

Contents

Week 1

1 - 1

It's always lively here.

Այստեղ միշտ աշխույժ է:

Aystegh misht ashkhuyzh e:

1 - 2

She glared at me.

Նա նայեց ինձ:

Na nayets' indz:

1 - 3

He's hurt his ankle.

Նա վնասել է իր կոճը:

Na vnasel e ir kochy:

1 - 4

Your table is ready.

Ձեր սեղանը պատրաստ է:

DZer seghany patrast e.

1 - 5

Ok, I'll take this one.

Լավ, ես կվերցնեմ սա:

Lav, yes kverts'nem sa:

1 - 6

I was moved to tears.

Ես հուզվեցի մինչև արցունքներս:

Yes huzvets'i minch'ev arts'unk'ners.

1 - 7

I'm sorry I'm late.

Կներես, որ ուշացել եմ:

Kneres, vor ushats'el yem:

Day 1

Week 1

2 - 1

Why did you go there?

Ինչո՞ւ գնացիր այնտեղ:

Inch'vo°w gnats'ir ayntegh.

2 - 2

I love my father.

Ես սիրում եմ հորս:

Yes sirum yem hors.

2 - 3

No, you cannot.

Ոչ, դուք չեք կարող:

Voch', duk' ch'ek' karogh:

2 - 4

Do I have to do it now?

Արդյո՞ք ես պետք է դա անեմ հիմա:

Ardyo°k' yes petk' e da anem hima:

2 - 5

I would rather go home.

Ես կգերադասեի տուն գնալ:

Yès kgeradasev tun gnal.

2 - 6

Is it useful?

Արդյո՞ք դա օգտակար է:

Ardyo°k' da ogtakar e:

2 - 7

Did anybody come?

Ինչ-որ մեկը եկել է?

Inch'-vor meky yekel e?

Day 2

Week 1

1/52

3 - 1

Alcohol is colorless.

Ալկոհոլը անգույն է:

Alkoholy anguyn e.

3 - 2

Who is he?

Ով է նա?

Ov e na?

3 - 3

Do not wet clean.

Մի թաց մաքրեք:

Mi t'ats' mak'rek':

3 - 4

He came here alone.

Նա այստեղ մենակ է եկել:

Na aystegh menak e yekel.

3 - 5

He's a soccer player.

Նա ֆուտբոլիստ է:

Na futbolist e:

3 - 6

I can't. I'm sorry.

Չեմ կարող: Կներես.

CH'em karogh. Kneres.

3 - 7

He is ten years old.

Նա տասը տարեկան է:

Na tasy tarekan e.

Day 3

Week 1

4 - 1

He's full of energy.

Նա լի է էներգիայով:

Na li e energiayov:

4 - 2

John, this is Mary.

Ջոն, սա Մերին է:

Jon, sa Merin e:

4 - 3

Would you mind?

Դեմ կլինես?

Dem klines?

4 - 4

She's good at makeup.

Նա լավ է դիմահարդարում:

Na lav e dimahardarum:

4 - 5

She loves to dance.

Նա սիրում է պարել:

Na sirum e parel.

4 - 6

I don't mind.

Ես դեմ չեմ:

Yes dem ch'em:

4 - 7

I watered the plant.

Ես ջրեցի բույսը:

Yes jrets'i buysy.

Day 4

Week 1

1/52

5 - 1

Sorry but we are full.

Կներեք, բայց մենք լցված ենք:

Knerek', bayts' menk' lts'vats yenk':

5 - 2

Birds flew southward.

Թռչունները թռան դեպի հարավ:

T'rrch'unnery t'rran depi harav.

5 - 3

He works hard every day.

Նա ամեն օր քրտնաջան աշխատում է:

Na amen or k'rtnajan ashkhatum e.

5 - 4

See you soon.

Կհանդիպենք շուտով:

Khandipenk' shutov:

5 - 5

I'm a little tired.

Ես մի քիչ հոգնած եմ:

Yes mi k'ich' hognats yem.

5 - 6

Is this seat taken?

Այս տեղը զբաղված է:

Ays teghy zbaghvats e:

5 - 7

I have a dull feeling.

Ես ձանձրալի զգացողություն ունեմ.

Yes dzandzrali zgats'voghut'yun unem.

Day 5

Week 1

1/52

6 - 1

I'm on holiday.
Ես արձակուրդում եմ:
Yes ardzakurdum yem.

6 - 2

Please stay as you are.
Խնդրում եմ մնա այնպիսին, ինչպիսին կաս:
Khndrum yem mna aynpisin, inch'pisin kas:

6 - 3

Read your books quietly.
Կարդացեք ձեր գրքերը հանգիստ:
Kardats'ek' dzer grk'ery hangist:

6 - 4

Put out the fire.
Հանգցնել կրակը:
Hangts'nel kraky:

6 - 5

He has a good heart.
Նա լավ սիրտ ունի:
Na lav sirt uni.

6 - 6

You can do it!
Դու կարող ես դա անել!
Du karogh yes da anel!

6 - 7

Can you hear me OK?
Կարո՞ղ ես ինձ լավ լսել:
Karo°gh yes indz lav lsel:

Day 6

Test 1

7 - 1

I was moved to tears.

7 - 2

I would rather go home.

7 - 3

He came here alone.

7 - 4

Would you mind?

7 - 5

Birds flew southward.

7 - 6

I'm on holiday.

7 - 7

Can you hear me OK?

Day 7

Week 2

8 - 1

I'm fine, thank you.

Լավ եմ, շնորհակալություն:

Lav yem, shnorhakalut'yun.

8 - 2

No, I'm serious.

Ոչ, ես լուրջ եմ ասում:

Voch', yes lurj yem asum:

8 - 3

What did you buy?

Ինչ եք գնել?

Inch' yek' gnel?

8 - 4

I can't stop vomiting.

Ես չեմ կարող դադարեցնել փսխումը:

Yes ch'em karogh dadarets'nel p'skhumy:

8 - 5

He doesn't smoke.

Նա չի ծխում:

Na ch'i tskhum:

8 - 6

He often watches movies.

Հաճախ է ֆիլմեր դիտում:

Hachakh e filmer ditum.

8 - 7

Please ask someone.

Խնդրում եմ, ինչ-որ մեկին հարցրեք:

Khndrum yem, inch'-vor mekin harts'rek':

Day 8

Week 2

9 - 1

We are open all day.

Մենք բաց ենք ամբողջ օրը:

Menk' bats' yenk' amboghj ory.

9 - 2

I am so stressed.

Ես այնքան լարված եմ:

Yes aynk'an larvats yem:

9 - 3

She was operated on.

Նրան վիրահատել են:

Nran virahatel yen.

9 - 4

That's not always true.

Դա միշտ չէ, որ ճիշտ է:

Da misht ch'e, vor chisht e:

9 - 5

Your hair is still wet.

Ձեր մազերը դեռ թաց են:

DZer mazery derr t'ats' yen:

9 - 6

I prefer tea to coffee.

Ես նախընտրում եմ թեյը սուրճից:

Yes nakhyntrum yem t'eyy surchits'.

9 - 7

Have you been abroad?

Եղե՞լ եք արտասահմանում:

Yeghe"l yek' artasahmanum:

Day 9

Week 2

10 - 1

Julia is my sister.

Ջուլիան իմ քույրն է:

Julian im k'uyrn e.

10 - 2

Read the paragraph.

Կարդացեք պարբերությունը.

Kardats'ek' parberut'yuny.

10 - 3

Please help me out sir.

Խնդրում եմ օգնեք ինձ պարոն:

Khndrum yem ognek' indz paron:

10 - 4

I'd be happy to.

Ես ուրախ կլինեմ:

Yes urakh klinem:

10 - 5

Please have your seat.

Խնդրում եմ նստեք ձեր տեղը:

Khndrum yem nstek' dzer teghy:

10 - 6

Remind me.

Հիշեցրու ինձ.

Hishets'ru indz.

10 - 7

Please wear slippers.

Խնդրում ենք հագնել հողաթափեր:

Khndrum yenk' hagnel hoghat'ap'er:

Day 10

Week 2

11 - 1

What's wrong?

Ինչ է պատահել?

Inch' e patahel?

11 - 2

Your skirt is rumpled.

Ձեր կիսաշրջազգեստը ճմլված է:

DZer kisashrjazgesty chmlvats e.

11 - 3

Practice first aid.

Կատարեք առաջին օգնություն.

Katarek' arrajin ognut'yun.

11 - 4

Meet me tomorrow.

Հանդիպեք ինձ վաղը:

Handipek' indz vaghy:

11 - 5

He's changed a lot.

Նա շատ է փոխվել:

Na shat e p'vokhvel:

11 - 6

I like reading books.

Ես սիրում եմ գրքեր կարդալ:

Yes sirum yem grk'er kardal.

11 - 7

He is fine.

Նա լավ է:

Na lav e.

Day 11

Week 2

12 - 1

Where did you meet him?

Որտեղ եք հանդիպել նրան:

Vortegh yek' handipel nran:

12 - 2

I am really cold.

Ես իսկապես մրսում եմ:

Yes iskapes mrsum yem.

12 - 3

We have plenty of time.

Մենք բավական ժամանակ ունենք:

Menk' bavakan zhamanak unenk':

12 - 4

It's too tight for me.

Ինձ համար դա չափազանց նեղ է:

Indz hamar da ch'ap'azants' negh e:

12 - 5

He has high ideals.

Նա բարձր իդեալներ ունի:

Na bardzr idealner uni.

12 - 6

How old is your son?

Քանի՞ տարեկան է քո որդին:

K'ani° tarekan e k'vo vordin.

12 - 7

She had surgery.

Նա վիրահատվել էր:

Na virahatvel er.

Day 12

Week 2

13 - 1

Did he say anything?

Ինչ-որ բան ասե՞լ է:

Inch'-vor ban ase՞l e.

13 - 2

Will you marry me?

Կամուսնանա՞ս ինձ հետ:

Kamusnana՞s indz het.

13 - 3

Don't panic.

Խուճապի մի մատնվեք:

Khuchapi mi matnvek':

13 - 4

Hi! How are you doing?

Ողջու՜յն! Ինչպես ես?

Voghju՜yn! Inch'pes yes?

13 - 5

I'm lost.

Ես կորել եմ.

Yes korel yem.

13 - 6

I am bold.

Ես համարձակ եմ.

Yes hamardzak yem.

13 - 7

This pipe is clogged.

Այս խողովակը խցանված է:

Ays khoghovaky khts'anvats e:

Day 13

Test 2

14 - 1

He often watches movies.

2/52

14 - 2

Your hair is still wet.

14 - 3

I'd be happy to.

14 - 4

Practice first aid.

14 - 5

I am really cold.

14 - 6

Did he say anything?

14 - 7

This pipe is clogged.

Day 14

Week 3

3/52

15 - 1

It's almost time.

Գրեթե ժամանակն է:

Gret'e zhamanakn e:

15 - 2

I have a headache.

Ես գլխացավ ունեմ.

Yes glkhats'av unem.

15 - 3

My room is rectangular.

Իմ սենյակն ուղղանկյուն է:

Im senyakn ughghankyun e.

15 - 4

How does it work?

Ինչպես է դա աշխատում?

Inch'pes e da ashkhatum?

15 - 5

I'm thirsty.

Ես ծարավ եմ.

Yes tsarav yem.

15 - 6

He could not come today.

Այսոր նա չկարողացավ գալ:

Aysor na ch'karoghats'av gal.

15 - 7

Please try this dish.

Խնդրում ենք փորձել այս ուտեստը:

Khndrum yenk' p'vordzel ays utesty:

Day 15

Week 3

16 - 1

Safe trip!

Անվտանգ է ուղեւորությունը!

Anvtang e ughevorut'yuny!

16 - 2

Please call this number.

Խնդրում ենք զանգահարել այս համարով:

Khndrum yenk' zangaharel ays hamarov.

16 - 3

What's up?

Ինչ կա?

Inch' ka?

16 - 4

I was locked up.

Ես փակված էի:

Yes p'akvats ei.

16 - 5

That would be fantastic!

Դա ֆանտաստիկ կլիներ:

Da fantastik kliner:

16 - 6

I admired his patience.

Ես հիանում էի նրա համբերությամբ:

Yes hianum ei nra hamberut'yamb.

16 - 7

He is frequently late.

Նա հաճախ է ուշանում:

Na hachakh e ushanum.

Day 16

Week 3

3/52

17 - 1

I hate carrots.

Ես ատում եմ գազարը:

Yes atum yem gazary.

17 - 2

What is your hobby?

Ո՞րն է քո հոբբին:

VO"rn e k'vo hobbin:

17 - 3

You look great.

Շատ լավ տեսք ունեք.

Shat lav tesk' unek'.

17 - 4

I am Mary.

Ես Մերին եմ:

Yes Merin yem.

17 - 5

Good evening.

Բարի երեկո.

Bari yereko.

17 - 6

Please take me along.

Խնդրում եմ ինձ հետ տարեք:

Khndrum yem indz het tarek':

17 - 7

Close your eyes.

Փակիր քո աչքերը.

P'akir k'vo ach'k'ery.

Day 17

Week 3

18 - 1

The sky's gray today.

Երկինքն այսոր մոխրագույն է:

Yerkink'n aysor mokhraguyn e:

18 - 2

I hope they will win.

Հուսով եմ՝ նրանք կհաղթեն:

Husov yem` nrank' khaght'en.

18 - 3

He scored three goals.

Նա երեք գոլ խփեց:

Na yerek' gol khp'ets'.

18 - 4

I'm thirty.

Ես երեսուն եմ:

Yes yeresun yem:

18 - 5

You're right.

Դու ճիշտ ես.

Du chishl yes.

18 - 6

Dry flat in shade.

Չորացնել հարթ ստվերում:

Ch'vorats'nel hart' stverum:

18 - 7

Let me help you.

Թույլ տվեք օգնել ձեզ:

T'uyl tvek' ognel dzez:

Day 18

Week 3

3/52

19 - 1

Don't skip meals.

Մի բաց թողեք կերակուրները:

Mi bats' t'voghek' kerakurnery:

19 - 2

For how many persons?

Քանի՞ անձի համար:

K'ani" andzi hamar:

19 - 3

The water is soft.

Ջուրը փափուկ է:

Jury p'ap'uk e.

19 - 4

I have a student visa.

Ունեմ ուսանողական վիզա:

Unem usanoghakan viza.

19 - 5

The air is clean here.

Այստեղ օրը մաքուր է:

Aystegh ody mak'ur e.

19 - 6

Too bad.

Շատ վատ.

Shat vat.

19 - 7

When is the next train?

Երբ է մեկնում հաջորդ գնացքը:

Yerb e meknum hajord gnats'k'y:

Day 19

Week 3

20 - 1

I've fully recovered.
Ես լիովին ապաքինվել եմ:
Yes liovin apak'invel yem:

3/52

20 - 2

Glad to meet you.
Ուրախ եմ հանդիպել ձեզ:
Urakh yem handipel dzez:

20 - 3

He is my husband.
Նա իմ ամուսինն է:
Na im amusinn e.

20 - 4

Let's begin.
Եկեք սկսենք.
Yekek' sksenk'.

20 - 5

Remember the date.
Հիշեք ամսաթիվը:
Hishek' amsat'ivy:

20 - 6

He's greedy for money.
Նա ագահ է փողի համար:
Na agah e p'voghi hamar:

20 - 7

It's for a present.
Դա նվերի համար է:
Da nveri hamar e:

Day 20

Test 3

21 - 1

He could not come today.

21 - 2

That would be fantastic!

21 - 3

I am Mary.

21 - 4

He scored three goals.

21 - 5

For how many persons?

21 - 6

I've fully recovered.

21 - 7

It's for a present.

Day 21

Week 4

22 - 1

He's courageous.

Նա համարձակ է:

Na hamardzak e:

4/52

22 - 2

We drink tea every day.

Մենք ամեն օր թեյ ենք խմում:

Menk' amen or t'ey yenk' khmum.

22 - 3

What do you recommend?

Ի՞նչ խորհուրդ կտաք?

Inch' khorhurd ktak'?

22 - 4

This work is hard.

Այս աշխատանքը ծանր է:

Ays ashkhatank'y tsanr e.

22 - 5

He was overtaking.

Նա շրջանցում էր:

Nu shrjants'um er.

22 - 6

He majors in physics.

Նա մասնագիտանում է ֆիզիկայից:

Na masnagitanum e fizikayits'.

22 - 7

Please give me that one.

Խնդրում եմ, տուր ինձ այդ մեկը:

Khndrum yem, tur indz ayd meky:

Day 22

Week 4

23 - 1

This sofa feels good.

Այս բազմոցը լավ է զգում:

Ays bazmots'y lav e zgum:

23 - 2

I didn't mean to.

Ես չէի ուզում:

Yes ch'ei uzum:

23 - 3

I have been mugged.

Ինձ գողացել են:

Indz goghats'el yen.

23 - 4

I jog every morning.

Ես ամեն առավոտ վազում եմ:

Yes amen arravot vazum yem:

23 - 5

It's a kind of fruit.

Դա մի տեսակ միրգ է:

Da mi tesak mirg e:

23 - 6

I belong to Oxford.

Ես պատկանում եմ Օքսֆորդին:

Yes patkanum yem Ok'sfordin.

23 - 7

Please eat.

Խնդրում եմ, կերեք:

Khndrum yem, kerek'.

Day 23

Week 4

24 - 1

Cool down.

Հանգստանալ.

Hangstanal.

24 - 2

I love lobsters.

Ես սիրում եմ օմար:

Yes sirum yem omar:

24 - 3

I don't get it.

Չեմ հասկանում:

CH'em haskanum:

24 - 4

I got sand in my shoes.

Կոշիկներիս մեջ ավազ եմ ստացել:

Koshikneris mej avaz yem stats'el.

24 - 5

He used to be poor.

Նա նախկինում աղքատ էր:

Na nakhkinum aghk'at er.

24 - 6

This match is a draw.

Այս հանդիպումը ոչ-ոքի է.

Ays handipumy voch'-vok'i e.

24 - 7

This juice is too sweet.

Այս հյութը չափազանց քաղցր է:

Ays hyut'y ch'ap'azants' k'aghts'r e:

Day 24

Week 4

25 - 1

Can I have one?

Կարո՞ղ եմ ունենալ մեկը:

Karo°gh yem unenal meky:

25 - 2

No, I don't mind.

Ոչ, ես դեմ չեմ:

Voch', yes dem ch'em:

25 - 3

What size do you wear?

Ի՞նչ չափսի եք հագնում:

Inch' ch'ap'si yek' hagnum:

25 - 4

He likes spicy food.

Նա սիրում է կծու սնունդ:

Na sirum e ktsu snund.

25 - 5

I'll pay for that.

Ես դրա համար կվճարեմ:

Yes dra hamar kvcharem.

25 - 6

Does he act well?

Նա լա՞վ է վարվում:

Na la°v e varvum.

25 - 7

Hello everyone.

Ողջույն բոլորին.

Voghjuyn bolorin.

Day 25

Week 4

26 - 1

The meat is cooked.

Միսը եփում է:

Misy yep'um e.

26 - 2

He is my neighbour.

Նա իմ հարևանն է:

Na im harevann e.

26 - 3

Follow this road.

Հետևեք այս ճանապարհին:

Hetevek' ays chanaparhin:

26 - 4

Violence is wrong.

Բռնությունը սխալ է.

Brrnut'yuny skhal e.

26 - 5

Please imitate my move.

Խնդրում եմ ընդօրինակեք իմ քայլը:

Khndrum yem yndorinakek' im k'ayly.

26 - 6

A double bed, please.

Երկտեղանոց մահճակալ, խնդրում եմ:

Yerkteghanots' mahchakal, khndrum yem:

26 - 7

He loves barbecues.

Նա խորոված է սիրում:

Na khorovats e sirum.

Day 26

Week 4

4/52

27 - 1

You're hired.
Դուք աշխատանքի եք ընդունվել:
Duk' ashkhatank'i yek' yndunvel:

27 - 2

What a beautiful house!
Ի՞նչ գեղեցիկ տուն է:
I¯nch' geghets'ik tun e.

27 - 3

She injured her arm.
Նա վնասել է ձեռքը:
Na vnasel e dzerrk'y.

27 - 4

My son brought a friend.
Տղաս ընկեր է բերել.
Tghas ynker e berel.

27 - 5

He is my colleague.
Նա իմ գործընկերն է:
Na im gortsynkern e.

27 - 6

How many hours drive?
Քանի ժամ մեքենայով:
K'ani zham mek'enayov:

27 - 7

It's too big for me.
Դա չափազանց մեծ է ինձ համար:
Da ch'ap'azants' mets e indz hamar:

Day 27

Test 4

28 - 1

He majors in physics.

4/52

28 - 2

It's a kind of fruit.

28 - 3

I got sand in my shoes.

28 - 4

What size do you wear?

28 - 5

He is my neighbour.

28 - 6

You're hired.

28 - 7

It's too big for me.

Day 28

Week 5

5/52

29 - 1

She has lots of clothes.

Նա շատ հագուստ ունի:

Na shat hagust uni:

29 - 2

She loves festivals.

Նա սիրում է փառատոներ:

Na sirum e p'arratoner:

29 - 3

It's very nice of you.

Շատ հաճելի է քո կողմից:

Shat hacheli e k'vo koghmits':

29 - 4

How did he come?

Ինչպե՞ս նա եկավ:

Inch'pe՞s na yekav:

29 - 5

The teacher guides us.

Ուսուցիչը մեզ ուղղորդում է.

Usuts'ich'y mez ughghordum e.

29 - 6

I met her in the town.

Ես նրան հանդիպեցի քաղաքում:

Yes nran handipets'i k'aghak'um:

29 - 7

I apologize for.

Ես ներողություն եմ խնդրում:

Yes neroghut'yun yem khndrum:

Day 29

Week 5

30 - 1

My name is John.

Իմ անունը Ջոն է.

Im anuny Jon e.

30 - 2

This car is very fast.

Այս մեքենան շատ արագ է:

Ays mek'enan shat arag e.

30 - 3

How's it going?

Ինչպե՞ս է դա ընթանում:

Inch'pe°s e da ynt'anum:

30 - 4

Then, you.

Հետո դու.

Heto du.

30 - 5

His crime is serious.

Նրա հանցանքը ծանր է:

Nra hants'ank'y tsanr e.

30 - 6

When were you born?

Երբ ես ծնվել?

Yerb yes tsnvel?

30 - 7

Are you angry with me?

Դուք բարկանո՞ւմ եք ինձ վրա:

Duk' barkano°wm yek' indz vra.

Day 30

Week 5

5/52

31 - 1

Watch your mouth.

Դիտեք ձեր բերանը.

Ditek' dzer berany.

31 - 2

I have a toothache.

Իմ ատամը ցավում է.

Im atamy ts'avum e.

31 - 3

It is direct?

Դա ուղիղ է?

Da ughigh e?

31 - 4

I'm home.

Ես տանն եմ.

Yes tann yem.

31 - 5

Let's pay separately.

Եկեք վճարենք առանձին:

Yekek' vcharenk' arrandzin:

31 - 6

Did it rain there?

Այնտեղ անձրև եկավ:

Ayntegh andzrev yekav.

31 - 7

Enjoy your stay!

Վայելեք ձեր հանգիստը:

Vayelek' dzer hangisty:

Day 31

Week 5

32 - 1

No, I did not do it.

Ոչ, ես դա չեմ արել:

Voch', yes da ch'em arel.

32 - 2

Draw a big circle there.

Այնտեղ գծեք մեծ շրջանակ:

Ayntegh gtsek' mets shrjanak:

32 - 3

No smoking.

Չծխել.

Ch'tskhel.

32 - 4

Is your wife employed?

Ձեր կինը զբաղվա՞ծ է:

DZer kiny zbaghvats e.

32 - 5

He mumbled to himself.

Նա ինքն իրեն փնթփնթաց.

Na ink n iren p'nt'p nt'ats'.

32 - 6

First aid center.

Առաջին օգնության կենտրոն.

Arrajin ognut'yan kentron.

32 - 7

Who would like to read?

Ո՞վ կցանկանար կարդալ:

VOv kts'ankanar kardal:

Day 32

Week 5

5/52

33 - 1

My mother was crying.

Մայրս լաց էր լինում:

Mayrs lats' er linum.

33 - 2

These shoes fit me.

Այս կոշիկներն ինձ սազում են:

Ays koshiknern indz sazum yen:

33 - 3

That's a good idea.

Լավ միտք է.

Lav mitk' e.

33 - 4

How old are you?

Քանի տարեկան ես?

K'ani tarekan yes?

33 - 5

He's sometimes late.

Նա երբեմն ուշանում է:

Na yerbemn ushanum e:

33 - 6

I will take a bath.

Ես լողանալու եմ:

Yes loghanalu yem.

33 - 7

Call the nurse.

Զանգահարեք բուժքրոջը:

Zangaharek' buzhk'rojy:

Day 33

Week 5

34 - 1

Describe yourself.

Նկարագրեք Ձեզ.

Nkaragrek' DZez.

34 - 2

He doesn't have time.

Նա ժամանակ չունի:

Na zhamanak ch'uni.

34 - 3

I feel feverish.

Ես զգում եմ ջերմություն:

Yes zgum yem jermut'yun:

34 - 4

I completely agree.

Լիովին համաձայն եմ:

Liovin hamadzayn yem.

34 - 5

It's been too long.

Շատ երկար է անցել:

Shat yerkar e ants'el:

34 - 6

Please stop joking.

Խնդրում եմ դադարեք կատակել:

Khndrum yem dadarek' katakel.

34 - 7

How is your sister?

Ինչպե՞ս է քույրդ:

Inch'pe°s e k'uyrd.

Day 34

Test 5

35 - 1

I met her in the town.

5/52

35 - 2

His crime is serious.

35 - 3

I'm home.

35 - 4

No smoking.

35 - 5

These shoes fit me.

35 - 6

Describe yourself.

35 - 7

How is your sister?

Day 35

Week 6

36 - 1

Challenge yourself.

Մարտահրավեր նետեք ինքներդ ձեզ:

Martahraver netek' ink'nerd dzez:

36 - 2

In my opinion.

Իմ կարծիքով.

Im kartsik'ov.

36 - 3

I'll be glad to do so.

Ես ուրախ կլինեմ դա անել:

Yes urakh klinem da anel:

36 - 4

She's a fashion expert.

Նա նորաձևության փորձագետ է:

Na noradzevut'yan p'vordzaget e:

36 - 5

How do I go about?

Ինչպե՞ս վարվեմ:

Inch'pe°s varvem:

36 - 6

I am John.

Ես Ջոնն եմ:

Yes Jonn yem:

36 - 7

Where is the baker's?

Որտեղ է հացթուխը:

Vortegh e hats't'ukhy:

Day 36

Week 6

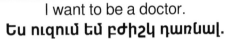

6/52

37 - 1

I want to be a doctor.

Ես ուզում եմ բժիշկ դառնալ.

Yes uzum yem bzhishk darrnal.

37 - 2

We sang loudly.

Մենք բարձր երգեցինք:

Menk' bardzr yergets'ink'.

37 - 3

I tripped on a stone.

Ես սայթաքեցի քարի վրա.

Yes sayt'ak'ets'i k'ari vra.

37 - 4

Today is my birthday.

Այսոր իմ ծննդյան օրն է.

Aysor im tsnndyan orn e.

37 - 5

I want to live abroad.

Ես ուզում եմ ապրել արտասահմանում.

Yes uzum yem aprel artasahmanum.

37 - 6

Merry Christmas!.

Շնորհավոր Սուրբ Ծնունդ!.

Shnorhavor Surb Tsnund!.

37 - 7

Let's meet this evening.

Եկեք հանդիպենք այսոր երեկոյան:

Yekek' handipenk' aysor yerekoyan:

Day 37

Week 6

38 - 1

What did you say?

Ինչ ասացիր?

Inch' asats'ir?

38 - 2

Please bend your knees.

Խնդրում եմ ծնկներդ ծալեք:

Khndrum yem tsnknerd tsalek'.

38 - 3

It was nobody's fault.

Ոչ ոքի մեղքը չէր:

Voch' vok'i meghk'y ch'er.

38 - 4

I had cookies and tea.

Ես թխվածքաբլիթներ և թեյ խմեցի:

Yes t'khvatsk'ablit'ner yev t'ey khmets'i:

38 - 5

With whom did you come?

ում հետ ես եկել?

Um het yes yekel?

38 - 6

When you've finished,

Երբ դու ավարտես,

Yerb du avartes,

38 - 7

I'm good at science.

Ես գիտության մեջ լավ եմ:

Yes gitut'yan mej lav yem:

Day 38

Week 6

6/52

39 - 1

Ask him not to go there.

Խնդրեք նրան չգնալ այնտեղ:

Khndrek' nran ch'gnal ayntegh:

39 - 2

How about water?

Ինչ կասեք ջրի մասին:

Inch' kasek' jri masin:

39 - 3

I ate a slice of cheese.

Ես կերա մի կտոր պանիր:

Yes kera mi ktor panir.

39 - 4

Many thanks.

Շատ շնորհակալություն.

Shat shnorhakalut'yun.

39 - 5

No big thing.

Ոչ մի մեծ բան:

Voch' mi mets ban:

39 - 6

How are you feeling?

Ինչպես ես քեզ զգում?

Inch'pes yes k'ez zgum?

39 - 7

I couldn't care less.

Ես չէի կարող անհանգստանալ:

Yes ch'ei karogh anhangstanal:

Day 39

Week 6

40 - 1

Can I open the windows?
Կարո՞ղ եմ բացել պատուհանները:

Karo°gh yem bats'el patuhannery:

40 - 2

Why did you beat him?
Ինչու՞ ես ծեծել նրան:

Inch'u° yes tsetsel nran:

40 - 3

Raise your pencils.
Բարձրացրեք ձեր մատիտները:

Bardzrats'rek' dzer matitnery:

40 - 4

His business failed.
Նրա բիզնեսը ձախողվեց:

Nra biznesy dzakhoghvets'.

40 - 5

Who are you?
Ով ես դու?

Ov yes du?

40 - 6

Why did he come?
Ինչու՞ նա եկավ:

Inch'u° na yekav:

40 - 7

Best wishes.
Լավագույն մաղթանքներով:

Lavaguyn maght'ank'nerov.

Day 40

Week 6

6/52

41 - 1

I am in pain.

Ես ցավ եմ ապրում.

Yes ts'av yem aprum.

41 - 2

She has special powers.

Նա ունի հատուկ լիազորություններ.

Na uni hatuk liazorut'yunner.

41 - 3

Don't move!

Մի՛ շարժվիր:

Mi˙ sharzhvir.

41 - 4

How do I?

Ինչպես կարող եմ?

Inch'pes karogh yem?

41 - 5

Will it rain today?

Այսօր անձրև կգա՞:

Aysor andzrev kga˚.

41 - 6

I can't believe that.

Ես չեմ կարող հավատալ դրան:

Yes ch'em karogh havatal dran:

41 - 7

Why are you asking me?

Ինչո՞ւ ես ինձ հարցնում:

Inch'vo˚w yes indz harts'num.

Day 41

Test 6

42 - 1

I am John.

42 - 2

I want to live abroad.

42 - 3

I had cookies and tea.

42 - 4

I ate a slice of cheese.

42 - 5

Why did you beat him?

42 - 6

I am in pain.

42 - 7

Why are you asking me?

Day 42

Week 7

43 - 1

He took off his glasses.

Նա հանեց ակնոցը:

Na hanets' aknots'y.

43 - 2

I hate the dentist.

Ես ատում եմ ատամնաբույժին.

Yes atum yem atamnabuyzhin.

43 - 3

I like wooden houses.

Ես սիրում եմ փայտե տներ:

Yes sirum yem p'ayte tner:

43 - 4

My passport is missing.

Անձնագիրս բացակայում է:

Andznagirs bats'akayum e.

43 - 5

He teaches mathematics.

Նա դասավանդում է մաթեմատիկա:

Na dasavandum e mat'ematika.

43 - 6

His driving is awful.

Նրա վարելը սարսափելի է:

Nra varely sarsap'eli e:

43 - 7

The dog licked my face.

Շունը լիզեց դեմքս:

Shuny lizets' demk's.

Day 43

Week 7

44 - 1

A handful of beans.

Մի բուռ լոբի:

Mi burr lobi.

44 - 2

This is a lonely song.

Սա միայնակ երգ է:

Sa miaynak yerg e.

44 - 3

I live in London.

Ես ապրում եմ Լոնդոնում.

Yes aprum yem Londonum.

44 - 4

It's very unlikely.

Շատ քիչ հավանական է:

Shat k'ich' havanakan e:

44 - 5

I am rather shy.

Ես բավականին ամաչկոտ եմ:

Yes bavakanın amach'kot yem.

44 - 6

Get enough sleep.

Բավականաչափ քնել:

Bavakanach'ap' k'nel:

44 - 7

Is service included?

Ծառայությունը ներառվա՞ծ է:

Tsarrayut'yuny nerarrva՞ts e:

Day 44

Week 7

45 - 1

Is she writing a letter?

Նա նամակ է գրում?

Na namak e grum?

7/52

45 - 2

Is there free Wi-Fi?

Կա՞ անվճար Wi-Fi:

Ka" anvchar Wi-Fi:

45 - 3

This pencil is sharp.

Այս մատիտը սուր է:

Ays matity sur e:

45 - 4

It's twelve thirty.

Ժամը տասներկու երեսուն է:

Zhamy tasnerku yeresun e.

45 - 5

All the best, bye.

Ամենայն բարիք, ցտեսություն:

Amenayn barik', ts'tesut'yun:

45 - 6

Can you play the piano?

Կարող եք դաշնամուր նվագել:

Karogh yek' dashnamur nvagel:

45 - 7

Did our client arrive?

Մեր հաճախորդը ժամանե՞լ է:

Mer hachakhordy zhamane"l e:

Day 45

Week 7

46 - 1

What time is my flight?

Ո՞ր ժամն է իմ թռիչքը։

VO՞r zhamn e im t'rrich'k'y:

46 - 2

My wallet is empty.

Իմ դրամապանակը դատարկ է։

Im dramapanaky datark e:

46 - 3

How was your flight?

Ինչպես անցավ թռիչքը?

Inch'pes ants'av t'rrich'k'y?

46 - 4

You're bleeding.

Դուք արյունահոսում եք։

Duk' aryunahosum yek':

46 - 5

I got up at seven today.

Այսօր յոթին վեր կացա։

Aysor yot'in ver kats'a.

46 - 6

Next, you.

Հաջորդը, դուք։

Hajordy, duk':

46 - 7

He finally showed up.

Նա վերջապես հայտնվեց։

Na verjapes haytnvets':

Day 46

Week 7

7/52

47 - 1

You're special to me.

Դու հատուկ ես ինձ համար:

Du hatuk yes indz hamar:

47 - 2

I don't eat salad.

Ես աղցան չեմ ուտում.

Yes aghts'an ch'em utum.

47 - 3

I need a green blouse.

Ինձ կանաչ բլուզ է պետք:

Indz kanach' bluz e petk'.

47 - 4

Hello! Do come in!

Բարեւ! Մտե՛ք

Barev! Mte'k'

47 - 5

This is my husband.

Սա իմ ամուսինն է:

Sa im amusinn e.

47 - 6

It will rain tomorrow.

Վաղը անձրև է գալու:

Vaghy andzrev e galu.

47 - 7

He's a good person.

Նա լավ մարդ է:

Na lav mard e:

Day 47

Week 7

48 - 1

He made her very angry.

Նա շատ զայրացրեց նրան:

Na shat zayrats'rets' nran.

48 - 2

Thank you very much.

Շատ շնորհակալություն.

Shat shnorhakalut'yun.

48 - 3

I rarely watch TV.

Ես հազվադեպ եմ հեռուստացույց դիտում:

Yes hazvadep yem herrustats'uyts' ditum:

48 - 4

My bike got a flat tire.

Իմ հեծանիվը պայթեց անվադողը:

Im hetsanivy payt'ets' anvadoghy:

48 - 5

The cake is too sweet.

Տորթը չափազանց քաղցր է:

Tort'y ch'ap'azants' k'aghts'r e:

48 - 6

He fulfilled my needs.

Նա կատարեց իմ կարիքները:

Na katarets' im karik'nery:

48 - 7

Did she appeal?

Նա բողոքարկե՞լ է:

Na boghok'arke°l e:

Day 48

Test 7

49 - 1

His driving is awful.

7/52

49 - 2

I am rather shy.

49 - 3

It's twelve thirty.

49 - 4

How was your flight?

49 - 5

I don't eat salad.

49 - 6

He made her very angry.

49 - 7

Did she appeal?

Day 49

Week 8

50 - 1

I don't think so.

Ես այդպես չեմ կարծում:

Yes aydpes ch'em kartsum.

50 - 2

She refused to attend.

Նա հրաժարվեց մասնակցել:

Na hrazharvets' masnakts'el:

50 - 3

You're kidding.

Դուք կատակում եք:

Duk' katakum yek':

50 - 4

It's clearly his fault.

Պարզ է, որ նրա մեղքն է:

Parz e, vor nra meghk'n e:

50 - 5

I have a backache.

Ես մեջքի ցավ ունեմ:

Yes mejk'i ts'av unem.

50 - 6

Excuse me.

Ներեցեք.

Nerets'ek'.

50 - 7

Please check the oil.

Խնդրում ենք ստուգել նավթը:

Khndrum yenk' stugel navt'y:

Day 50

Week 8

51 - 1

This whisky is strong.

Այս վիսկին ուժեղ է:

Ays viskin uzhegh e:

51 - 2

8/52

Take this road.

Գնացեք այս ճանապարհով:

Gnats'ek' ays chanaparhov:

51 - 3

How do you know that?

Դուք որտեղի՞ց գիտեք դա:

Duk' vorteghi"ts' gitek' da.

51 - 4

Don't lose your temper.

Մի կորցրեք ձեր ինքնատիրապետումը:

Mi korts'rek' dzer ink'natirapetumy:

51 - 5

Where do you come from?

Որտեղից ես գալիս?

Vorteghits' yes galis?

51 - 6

His teeth are white.

Նրա ատամներր սպիտակ են:

Nra atamnery spitak yen.

51 - 7

Does the water boil?

Ջուրը եռում է?

Jury yerrum e?

Day 51

Week 8

52 - 1

Thank you.

Շնորհակալություն.

Shnorhakalut'yun.

52 - 2

I have pain in my back.

Մեջքիս ցավեր ունեմ.

Mejk'is ts'aver unem.

52 - 3

This box is heavy.

Այս տուփը ծանր է:

Ays tup'y tsanr e:

52 - 4

It's hot.

Շոգ է:

Shog e.

52 - 5

Are you tired?

Հոգնա՞ծ ես?

Hognats yes?

52 - 6

Insert your pin code.

Տեղադրեք ձեր փին կոդը:

Teghadrek' dzer p'in kody:

52 - 7

I'm off work tomorrow.

Վաղը գործից դուրս եմ գալիս:

Vaghy gortsits' durs yem galis:

Day 52

Week 8

8/52

53 - 1

Mince the garlic.

Սխտորը մանրացնել:

Skhtory manrats'nel.

53 - 2

Open your books.

Բացեք ձեր գրքերը:

Bats'ek' dzer grk'ery:

53 - 3

I waited two days.

Երկու օր սպասեցի:

Yerku or spasets'i.

53 - 4

I feel very depressed.

Ես ինձ շատ ճնշված եմ զգում:

Yes indz shat chnshvats yem zgum.

53 - 5

Don't talk about that.

Մի խոսեք այդ մասին:

Mi khosek' ayd masin:

53 - 6

Put on your shirt.

Հագեք ձեր վերնաշապիկը:

Hagek' dzer vernashapiky:

53 - 7

I hate onions.

Ես ատում եմ սոխը:

Yes atum yem sokhy:

Day 53

Week 8

54 - 1

Stop here at red.

Կանգնեք այստեղ կարմիրի վրա:

Kangnek' aystegh karmiri vra:

54 - 2

I wrote him a letter.

Ես նրան նամակ գրեցի:

Yes nran namak grets'i.

54 - 3

She was born in Paris.

Նա ծնվել է Փարիզում:

Na tsnvel e P'arizum.

54 - 4

What was your first job?

Ո՞րն էր ձեր առաջին աշխատանքը:

VO°rn er dzer arrajin ashkhatank'y:

54 - 5

Best regards.

Հարգանքներով:

Hargank'nerov:

54 - 6

Please sit there.

Խնդրում եմ նստեք այնտեղ:

Khndrum yem nstek' ayntegh.

54 - 7

How are you?

Ինչպես ես?

Inch'pes yes?

Day 54

Week 8

8/52

55 - 1

Have a safe flight!

Անվտանգ թռիչք:

Anvtang t'rrich'k':

55 - 2

The earth is round.

Երկիրը կլոր է:

Yerkiry klor e.

55 - 3

I like this.

Հավանում եմ սա.

Havanum yem sa.

55 - 4

He is a national hero.

Նա ազգային հերոս է:

Na azgayin heros e.

55 - 5

My room is small.

Իմ սենյակը փոքր է:

Im senyaky p'vok'r e.

55 - 6

I beg your pardon.

Ներողություն.

Neroghut'yun.

55 - 7

My camera broke.

Տեսախցիկս կոտրվեց.

Tesakhts'iks kotrvets'.

Day 55

Test 8

56 - 1

Excuse me.

56 - 2

Where do you come from?

8/52

56 - 3

It's hot.

56 - 4

I waited two days.

56 - 5

I wrote him a letter.

56 - 6

Have a safe flight!

56 - 7

My camera broke.

Day 56

Week 9

57 - 1

He is out of town.
Նա քաղաքից դուրս է:
Na k'aghak'its' durs e.

57 - 2

Traffic light ahead.
Առջևում լուսացույց.
Arrjevum lusats'uyts'.

57 - 3

He is an unlikable man.
Նա անհավանական մարդ է:
Na anhavanakan mard e.

57 - 4

I was glad to meet him.
Ես ուրախ էի հանդիպել նրան:
Yes urakh ei handipel nran.

57 - 5

Sincerely thanks.
Անկեղծ շնորհակալություն:
Ankeghts shnorhakalut'yun:

57 - 6

Please turn this way.
Խնդրում եմ, թեքվեք այս կողմով:
Khndrum yem, t'ek'vek' ays koghmov:

57 - 7

I ordered a hamburger.
Ես համբուրգեր պատվիրեցի:
Yes hamburger patvirets'i.

Day 57

Week 9

58 - 1

Is she calling you?

Նա քեզ զանգո՞ւմ է:

Na k'ez zango°wm e:

58 - 2

The train door opened.

Գնացքի դուռը բացվեց:

Gnats'k'i durry bats'vets'.

58 - 3

Don't mention it.

Մի նշեք դա:

Mi nshek' da:

58 - 4

I believe you.

Ես հավատում եմ քեզ.

Yes havatum yem k'ez.

58 - 5

I am terribly sorry.

Ես սարսափելի ցավում եմ.

Yes sarsap eli ts'avum yem.

58 - 6

Are you ready?

Պատրաստ ես?

Patrast yes?

58 - 7

What date is today?

Ո՞ր օրն է այսօր:

VO°r orn e aysor:

Day 58

Week 9

9/52

59 - 1

He rides a motorcycle.
Նա մոտոցիկլետ է վարում:
Na motots'iklet e varum.

59 - 2

I'll take them all.
Ես բոլորին կվերցնեմ:
Yes bolorin kverts'nem:

59 - 3

Where is the station?
Որտեղ է կայանը:
Vortegh e kayany:

59 - 4

Could I use your phone?
Կարո՞դ եմ օգտագործել ձեր հեռախոսը:
Karo"gh yem ogtagortsel dzer herrakhosy:

59 - 5

Have a pizza.
Պիցցա խմեք:
Pits'ts'a khmek':

59 - 6

I'm really sorry.
Ես իսկապես ցավում եմ.
Yes iskapes ts'avum yem.

59 - 7

Welcome home.
Բարի գալուստ տուն.
Bari galust tun.

Day 59

Week 9

60 - 1

Please press the button.

Խնդրում ենք սեղմել կոճակը:

Khndrum yenk' seghmel kochaky:

60 - 2

Good luck.

Հաջողություն.

Hajoghut'yun.

60 - 3

Today is a holiday.

Այսօր տոն է:

Aysor ton e.

60 - 4

It was nothing really.

Դա իսկապես ոչինչ էր:

Da iskapes voch'inch' er:

60 - 5

When is your birthday?

Երբ է քո ծնունդը?

Yerb e k'vo tsnundy?

60 - 6

Buy one get one free.

Գնեք մեկը, ստացեք մեկը անվճար:

Gnek' meky, stats'ek' meky anvchar:

60 - 7

How is the weather like?

Ինչպե՞ս է եղանակը:

Inch'pe՞s e yeghanaky:

Day 60

Week 9

61 - 1

They shook hands.

Նրանք սեղմեցին ձեռքերը:

Nrank' seghmets'in dzerrk'ery.

9/52

61 - 2

Please turn left there.

Խնդրում եմ, թեքվեք ձախ այնտեղ:

Khndrum yem, t'ek'vek' dzakh ayntegh:

61 - 3

I forgave him.

Ես ներեցի նրան:

Yes nerets'i nran.

61 - 4

Do what you like.

Արա այն, ինչ քեզ դուր է գալիս:

Ara ayn, inch' k'ez dur e galis:

61 - 5

Where's the bank?

Որտեղ է բանկը:

Vortegh e banky:

61 - 6

It is already 8.30.

Արդեն 8.30 է:

Arden 8.30 e.

61 - 7

She's very pretty.

Նա շատ գեղեցիկ է:

Na shat geghets'ik e:

Day 61

Week 9

62 - 1

Where's the bookshop?

Որտեղ է գրախանութը:

Vortegh e grakhanut'y:

62 - 2

Does the dog bark?

Շունը հաչո՞ւմ է:

Shuny hach'vo"wm e.

9/52

62 - 3

This is very important.

Սա շատ կարևոր է:

Sa shat karevor e.

62 - 4

Sorry about that.

Ցավում եմ.

Ts'avum yem.

62 - 5

He is a fine poet.

Նա հիանալի բանաստեղծ է:

Na hianali banasteghts e:

62 - 6

He's off-guard.

Նա անվնաս է:

Na anvnas e:

62 - 7

I am friendly.

Ես ընկերասեր եմ:

Yes ynkeraser yem.

Day 62

Test 9

63 - 1

Please turn this way.

63 - 2

9/52

I am terribly sorry.

63 - 3

Could I use your phone?

63 - 4

Today is a holiday.

63 - 5

Please turn left there.

63 - 6

Where's the bookshop?

63 - 7

I am friendly.

Day 63

Week 10

64 - 1

I don't play any sports.

Ես ոչ մի սպորտով չեմ զբաղվում:

Yes voch' mi sportov ch'em zbaghvum.

64 - 2

Save for a rainy day.

Խնայեք անձրևոտ օրվա համար:

Khnayek' andzrevot orva hamar:

10/52

64 - 3

See you at 8 P.M.

Կհանդիպենք երեկոյան ժամը 8-ին:

Khandipenk' yerekoyan zhamy 8-in:

64 - 4

It's eleven o'clock.

Ժամը տասնմեկ է:

Zhamy tasnmek e.

64 - 5

Brilliant idea!

Փայլուն միտք!

P'aylun mitk'!

64 - 6

What time does it end?

Ժամը քանիսի՞ն է ավարտվում:

Zhamy k'anisi"n e avartvum:

64 - 7

Sure. Just a moment.

Իհարկե: Մեկ վայրկյան.

Iharke: Mek vayrkyan.

Day 64

Week 10

65 - 1

Where do I have to sign?

Որտե՞ղ պետք է ստորագրեմ։

Vorte"gh petk' e storagrem:

65 - 2

He knows my number.

Նա գիտի իմ համարը։

Na giti im hamary.

65 - 3

Please take notes.

Խնդրում եմ գրառումներ կատարել։

Khndrum yem grarrumner katarel:

65 - 4

I have strong teeth.

Ես ամուր ատամներ ունեմ։

Yes amur atamner unem.

65 - 5

Eat slowly.

Կերեք դանդաղ։

Kerek' dandagh:

65 - 6

Don't disturb me.

Ինձ մի խանգարեք։

Indz mi khangarek':

65 - 7

His father is a teacher.

Նրա հայրը ուսուցիչ է։

Nra hayry usuts'ich' e.

Day 65

Week 10

---

66 - 1

Who designed this one?

Ո՞վ է նախագծել այս մեկը:

VO"v e nakhagtsel ays meky:

---

66 - 2

Your bag is light.

Ձեր պայուսակը թեթև է:

DZer payusaky t'et'ev e:

10/52

---

66 - 3

Is everyone injured?

Բոլորը վիրավորվա՞ծ են:

Bolory viravorva"ts yen:

---

66 - 4

See you later.

Կտեսնվենք.

Ktesnvenk'.

---

66 - 5

You can try it.

Դուք կարող եք փորձել այն:

Duk' karogh yek' p'vordzel ayn:

---

66 - 6

A bird is flying.

Մի թռչուն է թռչում.

Mi t'rrch'un e t'rrch'um.

---

66 - 7

That's OK.

Դա նորմալ է.

Da normal e.

Day 66

Week 10

67 - 1

Could I speak to John?
Կարո՞ղ եմ խոսել Ջոնի հետ:
Karo°gh yem khosel Joni het:

67 - 2

He has gone out.
Նա դուրս է եկել:
Na durs e yekel.

67 - 3

No big deal.
Մեծ բան չէ.
Mets ban ch'e.

67 - 4

Dry in the shade.
Չորացնել ստվերում:
Ch'vorats'nel stverum.

67 - 5

What time is checkout?
Ո՞ր ժամն է վճարումը:
VO°r zhamn e vcharumy:

67 - 6

Ask him to call me.
Խնդրեք նրան զանգահարել ինձ:
Khndrek' nran zangaharel indz:

67 - 7

His company relocated.
Նրա ընկերությունը տեղափոխվեց:
Nra ynkerut'yuny teghap'vokhvets':

Day 67

Week 10

68 - 1

He's a very kind person.

Նա շատ բարի մարդ է:

Na shat bari mard e:

68 - 2

He slipped on the snow.

Նա սայթաքեց ձյան վրա:

Na sayt'ak'ets' dzyan vra.

68 - 3

Are they from abroad?

Դրսի՞ց են:

Drsi°ts' yen.

68 - 4

I like this show.

Ինձ դուր է գալիս այս շոուն:

Indz dur e galis ays shoun:

68 - 5

I love cats.

Ես սիրում եմ Կատուներ.

Yes sirum yem Katuner.

68 - 6

He came by car.

Նա մեքենայով եկավ:

Na mek'enayov yekav.

68 - 7

This is confidential.

Սա գաղտնի է:

Sa gaghtni e:

Day 68

Week 10

69 - 1

Return it safely.
Անվտանգ վերադարձրեք այն:

Anvtang veradardzrek' ayn:

69 - 2

He is busy as usual.
Նա սովորականի պես զբաղված է:

Na sovorakani pes zbaghvats e.

69 - 3

She's feminine.
Նա կանացի է:

Na kanats'i e:

69 - 4

It sounds good.
Լավ է հնչում:

Lav e hnch'um.

69 - 5

Yes, sir!
Այո պարոն!

Ayo paron!

69 - 6

Is she your sister?
Նա քո քո՞ւյրն է:

Na k'vo k'vo°wyrn e:

69 - 7

Your pulse is weak.
Ձեր զարկերակը թույլ է:

DZer zarkeraky t'uyl e.

Day 69

Test 10

70 - 1

What time does it end?

70 - 2

Eat slowly.

10/52

70 - 3

See you later.

70 - 4

No big deal.

70 - 5

He slipped on the snow.

70 - 6

Return it safely.

70 - 7

Your pulse is weak.

Day 70

Week 11

71 - 1

I go by scooter.

Ես գնում եմ սկուտերով:

Yes gnum yem skuterov:

71 - 2

11/52

He is a good cook.

Նա լավ խոհարար է:

Na lav khoharar e.

71 - 3

Get out of here!

Հեռացե՛ք այստեղից:

Herrats'e k' aysteghits'.

71 - 4

How much is this?

Որքա՞ն է սա:

Vork'aⁿn e sa:

71 - 5

Where is your house?

Որտեղ է ձեր տունը?

Vortegh e dzer tuny?

71 - 6

Is breakfast included?

Նախաճաշը ներառվա՞ծ է:

Nakhachashy nerarrvaⁿts e:

71 - 7

Use black ink only.

Օգտագործեք միայն սև թանաք:

Ogtagortsek' miayn sev t'anak':

Day 71

Week 11

72 - 1

It is very cold.

Շատ ցուրտ է.

Shat ts'urt e.

72 - 2

Please open the window.

Խնդրում եմ բացեք պատուհանը:

Khndrum yem bats'ek' patuhany.

72 - 3

Is it all true?

Այդ ամենը ճի՞շտ է:

Ayd ameny chi°sht e.

72 - 4

It was my pleasure.

Դա իմ հաճույքն էր:

Da im hachuyk'n er.

72 - 5

It's too expensive.

Դա չափազանց թանկ է:

Da ch'ap'azants' t'ank e:

72 - 6

My jaw hurts.

Ծնոտս ցավում է:

Tsnots ts'avum e.

72 - 7

How about you?

Իսկ դու ինչ կասես քո մասին?

Isk du inch' kases k'vo masin?

Day 72

Week 11

73 - 1

Don't doubt yourself.

Մի կասկածէք ինքներդ ձեզ.

Mi kaskatsek' ink'nerd dzez.

73 - 2

11/52

She is a youth icon.

Նա երիտասարդության պատկերակ է:

Na yeritasardut'yan patkerak e:

73 - 3

Have you got a computer?

Համակարգիչ ունե՞ք:

Hamakargich' une"k':

73 - 4

I took on a new job.

Ես նոր աշխատանքի անցա:

Yes nor ashkhatank'i ants'a.

73 - 5

Forget it.

Մոռացիր դա.

Morrats'ir da.

73 - 6

Please speak slowly.

Խնդրում եմ կամաց խոսեք:

Khndrum yem kamats' khosek'.

73 - 7

I uncorked the wine.

Ես բացեցի գինու խցանը:

Yes bats'ets'i ginu khts'any.

Day 73

Week 11

74 - 1

Do you have a sister?

Դուք քույր ունե՞ք։

Duk' k'uyr une°k'.

74 - 2

We studied democracy.

Մենք ուսումնասիրել ենք ժողովրդավարությունը. 11/52

Menk' usumnasirel yenk' zhoghovrdavarut'yuny.

74 - 3

Please come.

Խնդրում եմ արի։

Khndrum yem ari.

74 - 4

It's your fault.

Դա քո մեղքն է.

Da k'vo meghk'n e.

74 - 5

I like this bag.

Ինձ դուր է գալիս այս պայուսակը։

Indz dur e galis uys payusaky:

74 - 6

What is wrong with you?

Ինչ է եղել?

Inch' e yeghel?

74 - 7

Oh, that's terrible.

Օ՜, դա սարսափելի է։

O°, da sarsap'eli e:

Day 74

Week 11

75 - 1

Can you lift this table?

Կարող եք բարձրացնել այս սեղանը:

Karogh yek' bardzrats'nel ays seghany:

11/52

75 - 2

I have a big dream.

Ես մեծ երազանք ունեմ.

Yes mets yerazank' unem.

75 - 3

I study philosophy.

Սովորում եմ փիլիսոփայություն.

Sovorum yem p'ilisop'ayut'yun.

75 - 4

There are seven bananas.

Կան յոթ բանան:

Kan yot' banan:

75 - 5

Is she cutting a tree?

Նա ծառ է կտրում:

Na tsarr e ktrum:

75 - 6

She has blue eyes.

Նա կապույտ աչքեր ունի:

Na kapuyt ach'k'er uni:

75 - 7

Our cat had kittens.

Մեր կատուն ձագեր ուներ:

Mer katun dzager uner:

Day 75

Week 11

76 - 1

He's already gone home.

Նա արդեն տուն է գնացել:

Na arden tun e gnats'el:

76 - 2

She has a little son.

Նա ունի փոքրիկ որդի:

Na uni p'vok'rik vordi.

11/52

76 - 3

Where is the pilot?

Որտե˚ղ է օդաչուն:

Vorte˚gh e odach'un:

76 - 4

I go to a gym.

Ես գնում եմ մարզասրահ:

Yes gnum yem marzasrah:

76 - 5

Nobody can replace him.

Ոչ ոք չի կարող փոխարինել նրան:

Voch' vok' ch'i karogh p'vokharinel nran.

76 - 6

Whose mistake is it?

Ո˚ւմ սխալն է:

VO˚wm skhaln e:

76 - 7

He's a taxi driver.

Նա տաքսու վարորդ է:

Na tak'su varord e.

Day 76

Test 11

77 - 1

Is breakfast included?

77 - 2

It's too expensive.

11/52

77 - 3

I took on a new job.

77 - 4

Please come.

77 - 5

I have a big dream.

77 - 6

He's already gone home.

77 - 7

He's a taxi driver.

Day 77

Week 12

78 - 1

I want new shoes.
Ես ուզում եմ նոր կոշիկներ:
Yes uzum yem nor koshikner:

78 - 2

That's alright.
Դա լավ է:
Da lav e:

12/52

78 - 3

This pillow is too low.
Այս բարձը շատ ցածր է:
Ays bardzy shat ts'atsr e:

78 - 4

It was pouring today.
Այսոր հորդառատ էր:
Aysor hordarrat er.

78 - 5

Where's the library?
Որտեղ է գրադարանը:
Vortegh e gradarany:

78 - 6

He's rich.
Նա հարուստ է:
Na harust e:

78 - 7

Yes. Certainly.
Այո՛: Անշուշտ:
Ayo'. Anshusht.

Day 78

Week 12

12/52

79 - 1

Yes, please.

Այո խնդրում եմ.

Ayo khndrum yem.

79 - 2

This is a secret.

Սա գաղտնիք է:

Sa gaghtnik' e.

79 - 3

That would be okay.

Դա լավ կլիներ:

Da lav kliner:

79 - 4

I met her downtown.

Ես հանդիպեցի նրան քաղաքի կենտրոնում:

Yes handipets'i nran k'aghak'i kentronum:

79 - 5

Note the address.

Նշեք հասցեն.

Nshek' hasts'en.

79 - 6

This way please.

Այս կերպ խնդրում եմ:

Ays kerp khndrum yem:

79 - 7

I don't agree.

Ես համաձայն չեմ:

Yes hamadzayn ch'em.

Day 79

Week 12

80 - 1

Do you have a match?

Լուցկի ունե՞ք:

Luts'ki une°k':

80 - 2

Does he complain?

Նա բողոքո՞ւմ է:

Na boghok'vo°wm e.

80 - 3

She's a gorgeous woman.

Նա հիասքանչ կին է:

Na hiask'anch' kin e:

80 - 4

It was a nice evening.

Հաճելի երեկո էր:

Hacheli yereko er.

80 - 5

Friday would be perfect.

Ուրբաթ օրը կատարյալ կլիներ:

Urbat' ory kataryal kliner:

80 - 6

She likes traveling.

Նա սիրում է ճանապարհորդել:

Na sirum e chanaparhordel:

80 - 7

Get dressed quickly.

Շուտ հագնվեք:

Shut hagnvek'.

Day 80

Week 12

12/52

81 - 1

Where are my books?

Որտեղ են իմ գրքերը:

Vortegh yen im grk'ery:

81 - 2

Nice work.

Հաճելի աշխատանք:

Hacheli ashkhatank'.

81 - 3

Stop messing around.

Դադարեք խառնաշփոթը:

Dadarek' kharrnashp'vot'y:

81 - 4

He's still young.

Նա դեռ երիտասարդ է:

Na derr yeritasard e:

81 - 5

The ship is sinking.

Նավը խորտակվում է:

Navy khortakvum e.

81 - 6

No parking.

Կայանելը արգելված է.

Kayanely argelvats e.

81 - 7

What do you mean?

Ինչ ի նկատի ունես?

Inch' i nkati unes?

Day 81

Week 12

82 - 1

I'll give you this book.

Ես ձեզ կտամ այս գիրքը:

Yes dzez ktam ays girk'y:

82 - 2

He came here.

Նա եկավ այստեղ:

Na yekav aystegh.

12/52

82 - 3

He's good at singing.

Նա լավ է երգում:

Na lav e yergum:

82 - 4

How is the movie?

Ինչպես է ֆիլմը:

Inch'pes e filmy:

82 - 5

All right.

Լավ.

Lav.

82 - 6

He is very sensitive.

Նա շատ զգայուն է:

Na shat zgayun e.

82 - 7

Work in progress.

Աշխատանքն ընթացքի մեջ է.

Ashkhatank'n ynt'ats'k'i mej e.

Day 82

Week 12

83 - 1

Is the story true?

Պատմությունը ճի՞շտ է:

Patmut'yuny chi¨sht e.

83 - 2

She's with me.

Նա ինձ հետ է:

Na indz het e:

83 - 3

Can I get extra linen?

Կարո՞ղ եմ լրացուցիչ սպիտակեղեն ձեռք բերել:

Karo¨gh yem lrats'uts'ich' spitakeghen dzerrk' berel:

83 - 4

I'll pay in cash.

Կվճարեմ կանխիկ:

Kvcharem kankhik.

83 - 5

He ate rice in a bowl.

Բրինձ կերավ ամանի մեջ:

Brindz kerav amani mej.

83 - 6

I injured my thumb.

Վնասեցի բթամատս:

Vnasets'i bt'amats.

83 - 7

She is cold.

Նա մրսում է:

Na mrsum e:

Day 83

Test 12

84 - 1

He's rich.

84 - 2

Note the address.

12/52

84 - 3

It was a nice evening.

84 - 4

Stop messing around.

84 - 5

He came here.

84 - 6

Is the story true?

84 - 7

She is cold.

Day 84

Week 13

85 - 1

Is it raining?
Անձրև է գալիս:
Andzrev e galis:

13/52

85 - 2

No, thank you.
Ոչ, շնորհակալ եմ.
Voch', shnorhakal yem.

85 - 3

Your tickets, please.
Ձեր տոմսերը, խնդրում եմ:
DZer tomsery, khndrum yem:

85 - 4

He is not available.
Նա հասանելի չէ:
Na hasaneli ch'e.

85 - 5

I've got a sore throat.
Ես կոկորդի ցավ ունեմ:
Yes kokordi ts'av unem:

85 - 6

I can't get out.
Ես չեմ կարող դուրս գալ:
Yes ch'em karogh durs gal:

85 - 7

Well, shall we go?
Դե, գնանք?
De, gnank'?

Day 85

Week 13

86 - 1

I'm glad you like it.

Ուրախ եմ Ձեզ դուր է գալիս այն.

Urakh yem DZez dur e galis ayn.

86 - 2

Could you repeat?

Կարո՞ղ եք կրկնել:

Karo°gh yek' krknel:

86 - 3

He never keeps secrets.

Նա երբեք գաղտնիքներ չի պահում:

Na yerbek' gaghtnik'ner ch'i pahum.

86 - 4

It's Monday again.

Կրկին երկուշաբթի է:

Krkin yerkushabt'i e.

86 - 5

This dance is easy.

Այս պարը հեշտ է.

Ays pary hesht e.

86 - 6

Read them aloud.

Կարդացեք դրանք բարձրաձայն:

Kardats'ek' drank' bardzradzayn:

86 - 7

I'm scared of dogs.

Ես վախենում եմ շներից:

Yes vakhenum yem shnerits'.

Day 86

Week 13

87 - 1

No, thanks.

Ոչ, շնորհակալություն։

Voch', shnorhakalut'yun.

87 - 2

Who cares.

Ով մտածում է.

Ov mtatsum e.

13/52

87 - 3

She writes left-handed.

Նա գրում է ձախլիկ.

Na grum e dzakhlik.

87 - 4

This book is difficult.

Այս գիրքը դժվար է.

Ays girk'y dzhvar e.

87 - 5

I don't need a bag.

Ինձ պայուսակ պետք չէ։

Indz payusak petk' ch'e.

87 - 6

What do you see?

Ինչ ես դու տեսնում?

Inch' yes du tesnum?

87 - 7

Let's share more ideas.

Եկեք կիսվենք ավելի շատ գաղափարներով։

Yekek' kisvenk' aveli shat gaghap'arnerov:

Day 87

Week 13

88 - 1

3 is an odd number.

3-ը կենտ թիվ է:

3-y kent t'iv e.

88 - 2

I'll join you.

Ես կմիանամ քեզ:

Yes kmianam k'ez.

88 - 3

Are you sure about it?

Վստա՞հ եք դրանում:

Vsta°h yek' dranum.

88 - 4

Hold on tight.

ամուր բռնիր:

Amur brrnir.

88 - 5

All are fine.

Բոլորը լավ են:

Bolory lav yen.

88 - 6

Please come closer.

Խնդրում եմ մոտեցեք:

Khndrum yem motets'ek'.

88 - 7

Are you satisfied now?

Հիմա գո՞հ եք:

Hima go°h yek'.

Day 88

Week 13

89 - 1

His story was funny.

Նրա պատմությունը ծիծաղելի էր.

Nra patmut'yuny tsitsagheli er.

89 - 2

And I am good at it.

Եվ ես լավ եմ դրանում:

Yev yes lav yem dranum:

13/52

89 - 3

They are engaged.

Նրանք նշանված են:

Nrank' nshanvats yen.

89 - 4

Hybrid vehicles only.

Միայն հիբրիդային մեքենաներ:

Miayn hibridayin mek'enaner:

89 - 5

Show your solutions.

Ցույց տվեք ձեր լուծումները:

Ts'uyts' tvek' dzer lutsumnery:

89 - 6

No jumping.

Ոչ մի ցատկ:

Voch' mi ts'atk:

89 - 7

Are you following me?

Հետևո՞ւմ ես ինձ

Hetevo"wm yes indz

Day 89

Week 13

90 - 1

I can't afford it.
Ես չեմ կարող ինձ թույլ տալ դա:
Yes ch'em karogh indz t'uyl tal da:

90 - 2

It looks great on you!
Այն հիանալի տեսք ունի քեզ համար:
Ayn hianali tesk' uni k'ez hamar:

13/52

90 - 3

Shall I make tea?
Թեյ պատրաստե՞մ:
T'ey patraste°m.

90 - 4

Our cat is a male.
Մեր կատուն արու է:
Mer katun aru e.

90 - 5

This cake is yummy.
Այս տորթը համեղ է:
Ays tort y hâmegh e.

90 - 6

How is the new house?
Ինչպե՞ս է նոր տունը:
Inch'pe°s e nor tuny:

90 - 7

How old is the victim?
Քանի՞ տարեկան է զոհը:
K'ani° tarekan e zohy:

Day 90

Test 13

91 - 1

I can't get out.

91 - 2

This dance is easy.

13/52

91 - 3

This book is difficult.

91 - 4

Are you sure about it?

91 - 5

And I am good at it.

91 - 6

I can't afford it.

91 - 7

How old is the victim?

Day 91

Week 14

92 - 1

Where does he work?

Որտեղ է նա աշխատում:

Vortegh e na ashkhatum:

92 - 2

Don't you have a pen?

Գրիչ չունե՞ս:

Grich' ch'une˚s.

14/52

92 - 3

I sat in a window seat.

Ես նստեցի պատուհանի նստարանին:

Yes nstets'i patuhani nstaranin:

92 - 4

Thanks, I'll do it.

Շնորհակալություն, ես դա կանեմ:

Shnorhakalut'yun, yes da kanem:

92 - 5

The engine won't start.

Շարժիչը չի գործարկվի:

Sharzhich'y ch'i gortsarkvi:

92 - 6

Is the seat vacant?

Տեղը թափուր է?

Teghy t'ap'ur e?

92 - 7

Just stay there.

Պարզապես մնա այնտեղ:

Parzapes mna ayntegh:

Day 92

Week 14

93 - 1

He sold the house.

Նա վաճառեց տունը:

Na vacharrets' tuny.

93 - 2

Don't quarrel with him.

Մի վիճեք նրա հետ:

Mi vichek' nra het:

93 - 3

The answer is wrong.

Պատասխանը սխալ է.

Pataskhany skhal e.

93 - 4

What about you?

Իսչ կասես քո մասին?

Inch' kases k'vo masin?

93 - 5

Yes, I am certain.

Այո, համոզված եմ.

Ayo, hamozvats yem.

93 - 6

I love summer.

Ես սիրում եմ ամառը:

Yes sirum yem amarry.

93 - 7

Don't deceive people.

Մի խաբեք մարդկանց.

Mi khabek' mardkants'.

Day 93

Week 14

94 - 1

Anything to convey?
Ինչ-որ բան փոխանցելու:

Inch'-vor ban p'vokhants'elu:

94 - 2

I'm pleased to meet you.
Ես ուրախ եմ հանդիպել ձեզ:

Yes urakh yem handipel dzez:

14/52

94 - 3

My nose is stuffed up.
Քիթս լցված է:

K'it's lts'vats e.

94 - 4

That's wonderful.
Հրաշալի ~ է.

Hrashali ~ e.

94 - 5

He has big arms.
Նա մեծ ձեռքեր ունի:

Nu mets dzenk'er uni.

94 - 6

Sorry for my fault.
Կներեք իմ մեղքի համար:

Knerek' im meghk'i hamar:

94 - 7

You are welcome.
Խնդրեմ.

Khndrem.

Day 94

Week 14

95 - 1

Let's go over there.

Եկեք գնանք այնտեղ:

Yekek' gnank' ayntegh:

95 - 2

What do you want?

Ինչ ես դու ուզում?

Inch' yes du uzum?

14/52

95 - 3

He executed the plan.

Նա կատարեց ծրագիրը:

Na katarets' tsragiry.

95 - 4

He's just a drunkard.

Նա ուղղակի հարբեցող է:

Na ughghaki harbets'vogh e:

95 - 5

Have lunch.

Նախաճաշել.

Nakhachashel.

95 - 6

She has a lot of dolls.

Նա շատ տիկնիկներ ունի:

Na shat tiknikner uni:

95 - 7

Why are you late?

Ինչու ուշացար?

Inch'u ushats'ar?

Day 95

Week 14

96 - 1

She has fat legs.
Նա գեր ոտքեր ունի:
Na ger votk'er uni.

96 - 2

May I come in?
Կարող եմ ներս գալ?
Karogh yem ners gal?

14/52

96 - 3

He no longer hates her.
Նա այլևս չի ատում նրան:
Na aylevs ch'i atum nran:

96 - 4

I'll be back.
Ես կվերադառնամ.
Yes kveradarrnam.

96 - 5

Do not iron.
Մի արդուկեք:
Mi ardukek :

96 - 6

Say cheese!
Ասա պանիր!
Asa panir!

96 - 7

This flower smells good.
Այս ծաղիկը լավ հոտ է գալիս:
Ays tsaghiky lav hot e galis:

Day 96

Week 14

14/52

97 - 1

He is my father.

Նա իմ հայրն է.

Na im hayrn e.

97 - 2

I have no time.

Ժամանակ չունեմ.

Zhamanak ch'unem.

97 - 3

That sounds delicious!

Դա համեղ է հնչում:

Da hamegh e hnch'um:

97 - 4

Did you type the letter?

Դուք մուտքագրե՞լ եք նամակը:

Duk' mutk'agre"l yek' namaky:

97 - 5

The last step is.

Վերջին քայլն է.

Verjin k'ayln e.

97 - 6

Who is this man?

Ո՞վ է այս մարդը:

VO"v e ays mardy:

97 - 7

I am a vegetarian.

Ես բուսակեր եմ:

Yes busaker yem.

Day 97

Test 14

98 - 1

Is the seat vacant?

98 - 2

Yes, I am certain.

14/52

98 - 3

That's wonderful.

98 - 4

He executed the plan.

98 - 5

May I come in?

98 - 6

He is my father.

98 - 7

I am a vegetarian.

Day 98

Week 15

99 - 1

Do not drink.

Մի խմեք.

Mi khmek'.

99 - 2

I feel hungry.

Ես քաղց եմ զգում:

Yes k'aghts' yem zgum.

15/52

99 - 3

He came here yesterday.

Նա երեկ եկավ այստեղ:

Na yerek yekav aystegh.

99 - 4

Sure. Thank you.

Իհարկե: Շնորհակալություն.

Iharke: Shnorhakalut'yun.

99 - 5

She rarely gets angry.

Նա հազվադեպ է զայրանում:

Na hazvadep e zayranum:

99 - 6

He looked at me.

Նա նայեց ինձ.

Na nayets' indz.

99 - 7

It's been a while.

Որոշ ժամանակ է անցել:

Vorosh zhamanak e ants'el:

Day 99

Week 15

100 - 1

Please line up here.

Խնդրում ենք հերթագրվել այստեղ:

Khndrum yenk' hert'agrvel aystegh.

100 - 2

I feel very tired.

Ես ինձ շատ հոգնած եմ զգում:

Yes indz shat hognats yem zgum.

100 - 3

I got it.

Հասկացա.

Haskats'a.

100 - 4

This dish is tasteless.

Այս ուտեստն անհամ է:

Ays utestn anham e.

100 - 5

The moon is waxing.

Լուսինը աձում է:

Lusliny achnum e.

100 - 6

Swallows are flying.

Ծիծեռնակները թռչում են:

Tsitserrnaknery t'rrch'um yen.

100 - 7

So what?

Եւ ինչ?

Yev inch'?

Day 100

Week 15

101 - 1

I love cooking.

Ես սիրում եմ ճաշ պատրաստել:

Yes sirum yem chash patrastel.

101 - 2

My son is left-handed.

Տղաս ձախլիկ է.

Tghas dzakhlik e.

15/52

101 - 3

I'm going to undress.

Ես պատրաստվում եմ մերկանալ:

Yes patrastvum yem merkanal:

101 - 4

I feel thirsty.

Ես ծարավ եմ զգում:

Yes tsarav yem zgum.

101 - 5

Please forgive me.

Խնդրում եմ ներիր ինձ.

Khndrum yem nerir indz.

101 - 6

I'll go right away.

Ես անմիջապես կգնամ:

Yes anmijapes kgnam:

101 - 7

By all means.

Բոլոր միջոցներով.

Bolor mijots'nerov.

Day 101

Week 15

102 - 1

Are your equipment new?

Ձեր սարքավորումները նորությո°ւն են:

DZer sark'avorumnery norut'yo°wn yen:

102 - 2

He is rich but stingy.

Նա հարուստ է, բայց ժլատ:

Na harust e, bayts' zhlat.

15/52

102 - 3

May I know your name?

Կարո°ղ եմ իմանալ քո անունը:

Karo°gh yem imanal k'vo anuny:

102 - 4

Did you lock the door?

Դուռը կողպե°լ ես:

Durry koghpe°l yes.

102 - 5

I have office tomorrow.

Ես վաղը գրասենյակ ունեմ:

Yes vaghy grasenyak unem.

102 - 6

I can't help you.

Ես չեմ կարող քեզ օգնել:

Yes ch'em karogh k'ez ognel:

102 - 7

My husband is out now.

Ամուսինս հիմա դուրս է եկել:

Amusins hima durs e yekel:

Day 102

Week 15

103 - 1

I am fine and you?

Ես լավ եմ, իսկ դու?

Yes lav yem, isk du?

103 - 2

I accepted his opinion.

Ես ընդունեցի նրա կարծիքը:

Yes yndunets'i nra kartsik'y.

15/52

103 - 3

I got a full massage.

Ես լրիվ մերսում ստացա:

Yes lriv mersum stats'a.

103 - 4

All the best.

Ամենայն բարիք:

Amenayn barik'.

103 - 5

I work under pressure.

Ես աշխատում եմ ճնշման տակ.

Yes ashkhatum yem chnshman tak.

103 - 6

I haven't decided yet.

Դեռ չեմ որոշել:

Derr ch'em voroshel.

103 - 7

Please call me at home.

Խնդրում եմ զանգահարեք ինձ տանը:

Khndrum yem zangaharek' indz tany:

Day 103

Week 15

104 - 1

The server is down.

Սերվերը անջատված է։

Servery anjatvats e:

104 - 2

Her fingers are thin.

Նրա մատները բարակ են:

Nra matnery barak yen.

15/52

104 - 3

Are you in the queue?

Դուք հերթում եք:

Duk' hert'um yek':

104 - 4

Has anyone seen my bag?

Որևէ մեկը տեսե՞լ է իմ պայուսակը:

Voreve meky tese˚l e im payusaky:

104 - 5

She uses a wheelchair.

Նա հաշմանդամի սայլակ է օգտագործում:

Na hashmandami saylak e ogtagortsum.

104 - 6

His legs are short.

Նրա ոտքերը կարճ են:

Nra votk'ery karch yen.

104 - 7

She's wearing boots.

Նա կրում է կոշիկներ:

Na krum e koshikner:

Day 104

Test 15

105 - 1

He looked at me.

105 - 2

The moon is waxing.

105 - 3

I feel thirsty.

105 - 4

May I know your name?

105 - 5

I accepted his opinion.

105 - 6

The server is down.

105 - 7

She's wearing boots.

Day 105

Week 16

106 - 1

The sun is glaring.

Արևը շողշողում է:

Arevy shoghshoghum e:

106 - 2

He's studying now.

Նա հիմա սովորում է:

Na hima sovorum e.

106 - 3

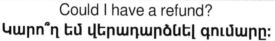

Could I have a refund?

Կարո՞ղ եմ վերադարձնել գումարը:

Karo°gh yem veradardznel gumary:

106 - 4

It is such a lovely day.

Այնքան սիրուն օր է:

Aynk'an sirun or e.

106 - 5

What's the matter?

Ի՞նչ է պատահել?

Inch' e patahel?

106 - 6

We're classmates.

Մենք դասընկերներ ենք:

Menk' dasynkerner yenk'.

106 - 7

It's ten o'clock.

Ժամը տաս է:

Zhamy tas e.

Day 106

Week 16

107 - 1

He turned the page.

Նա շրջեց էջը:

Na shrjets' ejy.

107 - 2

This orange is sour.

Այս նարինջը թթու է:

Ays narinjy t't'u e:

16/52

107 - 3

Please call a taxi.

Խնդրում եմ տաքսի զանգահարեք:

Khndrum yem tak'si zangaharek'.

107 - 4

She talks fast.

Նա արագ է խոսում:

Na arag e khosum:

107 - 5

Where do you work out?

Որտեղ եք մարզվում:

Vortegh yek' marzvum:

107 - 6

What do you do?

Ինչո՞վ եք զբաղվում:

Inch'vo˝v yek' zbaghvum.

107 - 7

Anything else?

Որևէ այլ բան?

Voreve ayl ban?

Day 107

Week 16

108 - 1

It's a waste of time.

Դա ժամանակի վատնում է:

Da zhamanaki vatnum e:

108 - 2

We played a video game.

Տեսախաղ խաղացինք:

Tesakhagh khaghats'ink'.

108 - 3

Who is not here today?

Ո՞վ այսոր այստեղ չէ:

VO"v aysor aystegh ch'e:

108 - 4

Whose book is this?

Ում գիրքն է սա?

Um girk'n e sa?

108 - 5

Pork is delicious.

Խոզի միսը համեղ է:

Khozi misy hamegh e.

108 - 6

She has two children.

Նա ունի երկու երեխա:

Na uni yerku yerekha.

108 - 7

Hi. I'm Cindy.

Ողջու՛յն. Ես Սինդին եմ:

Voghju"yn. Yes Sindin yem:

Day 108

Week 16

109 - 1

This one is cheaper.

Այս մեկն ավելի էժան է:

Ays mekn aveli ezhan e.

109 - 2

It does not fit my size.

Այն չի համապատասխանում իմ չափսին:

Ayn ch'i hamapataskhanum im ch'ap'sin:

109 - 3

Can I borrow a pencil?

Կարո՞ղ եմ մատիտ վերցնել:

Karo°gh yem matit verts'nel:

109 - 4

Let's meet on Monday.

Եկեք հանդիպենք երկուշաբթի օրը:

Yekek' handipenk' yerkushabt'i ory:

109 - 5

Sorry I am late.

Կներեք, որ ուշացել եմ:

Knerek', vor ushats'el yem.

109 - 6

Are you employed?

Դուք զբաղվա՞ծ եք:

Duk' zbaghva°ts yek'.

109 - 7

A table for two, please.

Սեղան երկուսի համար, խնդրում եմ:

Seghan yerkusi hamar, khndrum yem.

Day 109

Week 16

110 - 1

My friend got divorced.

Ընկերս ամուսնալուծվեց.

Ynkers amusnalutsvets'.

110 - 2

I'm sleepy.

Ես քնկոտ եմ.

Yes k'nkot yem.

110 - 3

How many people?

Ինչքան մարդ?

Inch'k'an mard?

16/52

110 - 4

It's cold in this room.

Այս սենյակում ցուրտ է:

Ays senyakum ts'urt e:

110 - 5

I dyed my hair red.

Մազերս կարմիր ներկեցի:

Mazers karmir nerkets'i.

110 - 6

It might rain today.

Այսօր հնարավոր է անձրև լինի:

Aysor hnaravor e andzrev lini:

110 - 7

Take a deep breath.

Խորը շունչ քաշիր.

Khory shunch' k'ashir.

Day 110

Week 16

16/52

111 - 1

Here is your change.

Ահա ձեր փոփոխությունը:

Aha dzer p'vop'vokhut'yuny.

111 - 2

With pleasure.

Հաձույքով.

Hachuyk'ov.

111 - 3

Where are you living?

Որտեղ ես դու ապրում?

Vortegh yes du aprum?

111 - 4

I feel powerful.

Ես ինձ հզոր եմ զգում:

Yes indz hzor yem zgum.

111 - 5

The team was weak.

Թիմը թույl էր.

T'imy t'uyl er.

111 - 6

Please don't be late.

Խնդրում եմ մի ուշացեք:

Khndrum yem mi ushats'ek'.

111 - 7

I was stuck in traffic.

Ես խցանվել էի երթեւեկության մեջ:

Yes khts'anvel ei yert'evekut'yan mej.

Day 111

Test 16

112 - 1

We're classmates.

112 - 2

Where do you work out?

112 - 3

Whose book is this?

16/52

112 - 4

Can I borrow a pencil?

112 - 5

I'm sleepy.

112 - 6

Here is your change.

112 - 7

I was stuck in traffic.

Day 112

Week 17

113 - 1

It is very far.

Շատ հեռու է:

Shat herru e.

113 - 2

I have some books.

Ես ունեմ մի քանի գրքեր:

Yes unem mi k'ani grk'er:

17/52

113 - 3

Bring them here.

Բերեք նրանց այստեղ:

Berek' nrants' aystegh:

113 - 4

What is this?

Ի՞նչ է սա?

Inch' e sa?

113 - 5

It tastes good!

Այն համով է!

Ayn hamov e!

113 - 6

Do not open.

Չբացել.

Ch'bats'el.

113 - 7

She saved a sick dog.

Նա փրկեց հիվանդ շանը.

Na p'rkets' hivand shany.

Day 113

Week 17

114 - 1

He didn't work hard.

Նա շատ չաշխատեց:

Na shat ch'ashkhatets'.

114 - 2

Is everything alright?

Ամեն ինչ կարգին է՞

Amen inch' kargin e?

114 - 3

I feel giddy.

Ես գլխապտույտ եմ զգում:

Yes glkhaptuyt yem zgum:

17/52

114 - 4

Mind the steps.

Ուշադրություն դարձրեք քայլերին.

Ushadrut'yun dardzrek' k'aylerin.

114 - 5

I am living in London.

Ես ապրում եմ Լոնդոնում:

Yes aprum yem Londonum.

114 - 6

We drank premium wine.

Մենք խմեցինք բարձրակարգ գինի:

Menk' khmets'ink' bardzrakarg gini.

114 - 7

Take care of yourself.

Խնայիր քեզ.

Khnayir k'ez.

Day 114

Week 17

115 - 1

He's a fine man.

Նա լավ մարդ է:

Na lav mard e:

115 - 2

He is on leave.

Նա արձակուրդում է:

Na ardzakurdum e.

115 - 3

Hello, can you hear me?

Բարև, լսու՞մ եք ինձ:

Barev, lsu"m yek' indz:

115 - 4

Does she behold me?

Նա տեսնու՞մ է ինձ:

Na tesnu"m e indz:

115 - 5

Forget the past.

Մոռացեք անցյալը.

Morrats'ek' ants'yaly.

115 - 6

Maximum occupancy.

Առավելագույն զբաղվածություն.

Arravelaguyn zbaghvatsut'yun.

115 - 7

Let's go home.

Եկեք գնանք տուն.

Yekek' gnank' tun.

Day 115

Week 17

116 - 1

Hi Jack. I'm Sophia.

Բարև Ջեկ: Ես Սոֆյան եմ:

Barev Jek: Yes Sofyan yem:

116 - 2

I will not buy it.

Չեմ գնի:

CH'em gni.

116 - 3

She is my mother.

Նա իմ մայրն է:

Na im mayrn e.

116 - 4

This is my sister.

Սա իմ քույրն է.

Sa im k'uyrn e.

116 - 5

I mended it.

Ես ուղղեցի այն:

Yes ughghets'i ayn:

116 - 6

Please open the door.

Խնդրում եմ բացեք դուռը:

Khndrum yem bats'ek' durry.

116 - 7

He's a loser.

Նա պարտվող է:

Na partvogh e:

Day 116

Week 17

117 - 1

My shirt is ripped up.
Իմ վերնաշապիկը պատռված է:
Im vernashapiky patrrvats e:

117 - 2

Please give me a minute.
Խնդրում եմ ինձ մի րոպե տվեք:
Khndrum yem indz mi rope tvek':

117 - 3

17/52

He lives around here.
Նա ապրում է այստեղ:
Na aprum e aystegh:

117 - 4

What a bad idea.
Ինչ վատ գաղափար է:
Inch' vat gaghap'ar e:

117 - 5

Keep cool.
Պահպանեք սառը:
Pahpanek' sarry:

117 - 6

I feel guilty.
Ես ինձ մեղավոր եմ զգում.
Yes indz meghavor yem zgum.

117 - 7

Did he borrow a pen?
Գրիչ վերցրե՞լ է:
Grich' verts're˚l e.

Day 117

Week 17

118 - 1

My back itches.

Մեջքս քոր է գալիս:

Mejk's k'vor e galis.

118 - 2

His voice is soft.

Նրա ձայնը մեղմ է.

Nra dzayny meghm e.

118 - 3

Don't lose your receipt!

Մի կորցրեք ձեր անդորրագիրը:

Mi korts'rek' dzer andorragiry:

17/52

118 - 4

My nose is itchy.

Քիթս քոր է գալիս:

K'it's k'vor e galis.

118 - 5

He speaks clearly.

Նա հստակ խոսում է.

Na hstak khosum e.

118 - 6

It's too late now.

Հիմա արդեն ուշ է:

Hima arden ush e.

118 - 7

A pitcher of beer.

Մի կուժ գարեջուր.

Mi kuzh garejur.

Day 118

Test 17

Do not open.

I am living in London.

17/52

Does she behold me?

She is my mother.

Please give me a minute.

My back itches.

A pitcher of beer.

Day 119

Week 18

120 - 1

What should I do?

Ի՞նչ պետք է անեմ։

Inch' petk' e anem?

120 - 2

That shirt looks cheap.

Այդ վերնաշապիկը էժան տեսք ունի։

Ayd vernashapiky ezhan tesk' uni.

120 - 3

Will you be my friend?

Կլինե՞ս իմ ընկերը։

18/52

Kline˚s im ynkery.

120 - 4

Can I try this on?

Կարո՞ղ եմ սա փորձել։

Karo˚gh yem sa p'vordzel:

120 - 5

Let's check your papers.

Եկեք ստուգենք ձեր թղթերը։

Yekek' stugenk' dzer t'ght'ery:

120 - 6

He is a Business Man.

Նա գործարար մարդ է։

Na gortsarar mard e:

120 - 7

Her baby is cute.

Նրա երեխան սրամիտ է։

Nra yerekhan sramit e:

Day 120

Week 18

121 - 1

He came by bus.

Նա ավտոբուսով եկավ:

Na avtobusov yekav.

121 - 2

I hear a strange sound.

Տարօրինակ ձայն եմ լսում.

Tarorinak dzayn yem lsum.

18/52

121 - 3

He spat on the ground.

Նա թքեց գետնին:

Na t'k'ets' getnin.

121 - 4

He loves himself.

Նա սիրում է իրեն:

Na sirum e iren.

121 - 5

I'm a terrible singer.

Ես սարսափելի երգիչ եմ:

Yes sarsap'eli yergich' yem:

121 - 6

My aunt lives in Madrid.

Հորաքույրս ապրում է Մադրիդում:

Horak'uyrs aprum e Madridum.

121 - 7

Excellent.

Գերազանց:

Gerazants'.

Day 121

Week 18

122 - 1

It's nice to meet you.

Հաճելի է հանդիպել քեզ:

Hacheli e handipel k'ez:

122 - 2

This food is tasteless.

Այս ուտելիքն անհամ է:

Ays utelik'n anham e.

122 - 3

I can help you.

Ես կարող եմ օգնել քեզ.

Yes karogh yem ognel k'ez.

18/52

122 - 4

Did I ask them to wait?

Ես նրանց խնդրե՞լ եմ սպասել:

Yes nrants' khndre"l yem spasel.

122 - 5

The bill, please.

Օրինագիծը, խնդրում եմ:

Orinagitsy, khndrum yem:

122 - 6

Are you being served?

Ձեզ սպասարկու՞մ են:

DZez spasarku"m yen.

122 - 7

I did it because of you.

Ես դա արեցի քո պատճառով:

Yes da arets'i k'vo patcharrov:

Day 122

Week 18

123 - 1

I need a lot of money.

Ինձ շատ փող է պետք:

Indz shat p'vogh e petk'.

123 - 2

Raise your hands.

Բարձրացրու ձերքերդ.

Bardzrats'ru dzerrk'erd.

18/52

123 - 3

It was a foggy night.

Մառախլապատ գիշեր էր:

Marrakhlapat gisher er.

123 - 4

We have an emergency.

Արտակարգ դեպք ունենք.

Artakarg depk' unenk'.

123 - 5

Why did he come here?

Ինչո՞ւ է նա եկել այստեղ:

Inch'vo°w e na yekel aystegh.

123 - 6

I just love summer.

Ես պարզապես սիրում եմ ամառը:

Yes parzapes sirum yem amarry:

123 - 7

My foot went numb.

Ոտքս թմրեց:

Votk's t'mrets'.

Day 123

Week 18

124 - 1

No food and drinks.

Սնունդ և խմիչք չկա:

Snund yev khmich'k' ch'ka:

124 - 2

A sack of rice.

Մի պարկ բրինձ.

Mi park brindz.

124 - 3

How late is it?

Որքա°ն է ուշ:

Vork'a°n e ush:

18/52

124 - 4

Is it serious?

Լո°ւրջ է:

Lo°wrj e.

124 - 5

Do you know that girl?

Դուք ճանաչու°մ եք այդ աղջկան:

Duk' chanach'u°m yek' ayd aghjkan.

124 - 6

I got a promotion today.

Ես այսոր առաջխաղացում ստացա:

Yes aysor arrajkhaghats'um stats'a:

124 - 7

It doesn't matter to me.

Ինձ համար դա նշանակություն չունի:

Indz hamar da nshanakut'yun ch'uni.

Day 124

Week 18

125 - 1

If only he were here!
Եթե միայն նա լիներ այստեղ:
Yet'e miayn na liner aystegh:

125 - 2

He's an actor.
Նա դերասան է:
Na derasan e.

18/52

125 - 3

Why didn't you come?
Ինչո՞ւ չեկար:
Inch'vo"w ch'ekar.

125 - 4

Absolutely.
Բացարձակապես:
Bats'ardzakapes.

125 - 5

Who are your bankers?
Ովքե՞ր են ձեր բանկիրները:
Ovk'e"r yen dzer bankirnery:

125 - 6

I took the first train.
Ես գնացի առաջին գնացքը:
Yes gnats'i arrajin gnats'k'y.

125 - 7

The stew burnt.
Այրվել է շողեխաշածը.
Ayrvel e shogekhashatsy.

Day 125

Test 18

126 - 1

He is a Business Man.

126 - 2

I'm a terrible singer.

126 - 3

Did I ask them to wait?

18/52

126 - 4

It was a foggy night.

126 - 5

A sack of rice.

126 - 6

If only he were here!

126 - 7

The stew burnt.

Day 126

Week 19

127 - 1

May I take a message?

Կարո՞դ եմ հաղորդագրություն վերցնել:

Karo°gh yem haghordagrut'yun verts'nel:

127 - 2

Now I've got to go.

Հիմա ես պետք է գնամ:

Hima yes petk' e gnam:

19/52

127 - 3

Please hurry!

Խնդրում եմ շտապե՛ք:

Khndrum yem shtape'k'.

127 - 4

Give it to them.

Տվեք նրանց:

Tvek' nrants':

127 - 5

I like dogs a lot.

Ես շատ եմ սիրում շներին:

Yes shat yem sirum shnerin.

127 - 6

Always wash your hands.

Միշտ լվացեք ձեր ձեռքերը:

Misht lvats'ek' dzer dzerrk'ery:

127 - 7

Please bring the chair.

Խնդրում եմ, բերեք աթոռը:

Khndrum yem, berek' at'vorry.

Day 127

Week 19

128 - 1

What station is it?

Ո՞ր կայանն է:

VO°r kayann e.

128 - 2

I'm against it.

Ես դեմ եմ դրան:

Yes dem yem dran.

128 - 3

No, I don't have one.

Ոչ, ես չունեմ:

Voch', yes ch'unem:

19/52

128 - 4

It was nice meeting you.

Հաճելի էր հանդիպել քեզ հետ:

Hacheli er handipel k'ez het:

128 - 5

Does he add wealth?

Նա հարստությո՞ւն է ավելացնում:

Na harstut'yo°wn e avelats num.

128 - 6

What a nice dress.

Ինչ լավ զգեստ է:

Inch' lav zgest e:

128 - 7

It's your mistake.

Դա քո սխալն է:

Da k'vo skhaln e.

Day 128

Week 19

129 - 1

That's all for today.

Այսօրվա համար այսքանը:

Aysorva hamar aysk'any:

129 - 2

I'm off on Thursday.

Հինգշաբթի օրը ես դուրս եմ գալիս:

Hingshabt'i ory yes durs yem galis:

19/52

129 - 3

I'll check.

Ես կստուգեմ.

Yes kstugem.

129 - 4

How is your mother?

Ինչպես է ձեր մայրը?

Inch'pes e dzer mayry?

129 - 5

His grades are not bad.

Նրա գնահատականները վատը չեն:

Nra gnahatakannery vaty ch'en.

129 - 6

I have a favor to ask.

Ես մի լավություն ունեմ խնդրելու.

Yes mi lavut'yun unem khndrelu.

129 - 7

What brand is that?

Ինչ ապրանքանիշ է դա:

Inch' aprank'anish e da:

Day 129

Week 19

130 - 1

How long will it take?

Որքան ժամանակ դա կպահանջի?

Vork'an zhamanak da kpahanji?

130 - 2

I marked the mistakes.

Ես նշել եմ սխալները.

Yes nshel yem skhalnery.

130 - 3

This is my teacher.

Սա իմ ուսուցիչն է:

Sa im usuts'ich'n e.

19/52

130 - 4

My father snores loudly.

Հայրս բարձր խռմփացնում է.

Hayrs bardzr khrrmp'ats'num e.

130 - 5

I am fine.

Ես լավ եմ.

Yes lav ynm.

130 - 6

She can speak Italian.

Նա կարող է խոսել իտալերեն:

Na karogh e khosel italeren:

130 - 7

He's a cunning man.

Նա խորամանկ մարդ է:

Na khoramank mard e:

Day 130

Week 19

131 - 1

He suddenly stood up.

Նա հանկարծ ոտքի կանգնեց։

Na hankarts votk'i kangnets'.

131 - 2

It's very gaudy.

Շատ շքեղ է։

Shat shk'egh e:

131 - 3

Why should I care?

Ինչու՞ պետք է հոգ տանեմ։

Inch'u" petk' e hog tanem:

131 - 4

Let's go slowly.

Եկեք կամաց գնանք։

Yekek' kamats' gnank':

131 - 5

She likes tall men.

Նրան դուր են գալիս բարձրահասակ տղամարդիկ։

Nran dur yen galis bardzrahasak tghamardik.

131 - 6

James is my husband.

Ջեյմսն իմ ամուսինն է։

Jeymsn im amusinn e.

131 - 7

Be aware of cyclists.

Զգուշացեք հեծանվորդներից։

Zgushats'ek' hetsanvordnerits':

Day 131

Week 19

132 - 1

I am a teacher.

Ես ուսուցիչ եմ:

Yes ususts'ich' yem.

132 - 2

She closed her eyes.

Նա փակեց աչքերը:

Na p'akets' ach'k'ery.

132 - 3

Can I give you a hand?

Կարո՞ղ եմ ձեզ ձեռք տալ:

Karo°gh yem dzez dzerrk' tal:

19/52

132 - 4

I was kidnapped.

Ինձ առևանգել էին:

Indz arrevangel ein.

132 - 5

Don't you have change?

Փոփոխություն չունե՞ք:

P'vop'vokhut'yun ch unē k'.

132 - 6

Attend to the phone.

Հաձախեք հեռախոսին.

Hachakhek' herrakhosin.

132 - 7

Sea water is salty.

Ծովի ջուրը աղի է:

Tsovi jury aghi e.

Day 132

Test 19

133 - 1

Always wash your hands.

133 - 2

Does he add wealth?

133 - 3

How is your mother?

19/52

133 - 4

This is my teacher.

133 - 5

It's very gaudy.

133 - 6

I am a teacher.

133 - 7

Sea water is salty.

Day 133

Week 20

134 - 1

Clean up your place.

Մաքրիր քո տեղը։

Mak'rir k'vo teghy.

134 - 2

Do as you like.

Արեք այնպես, ինչպես ցանկանում եք։

Arek' aynpes, inch'pes ts'ankanum yek':

134 - 3

Where is the bus stop?

Որտե՞ղ է կանգառը։

Vorte°gh e kangarry:

20/52

134 - 4

There's a bird flying.

Մի թռչուն է թռչում։

Mi t'rrch'un e t'rrch'um:

134 - 5

Can anyone hear me?

Որևէ մեկը կարող է ինձ լսել։

Voreve meky karogh e indz lsel:

134 - 6

What brings you here?

Ինչ է բերում ձեզ այստեղ?

Inch' e berum dzez aystegh?

134 - 7

I don't know for sure.

Ես հաստատ չգիտեմ։

Yes hastat ch'gitem.

Day 134

Week 20

135 - 1

I need car insurance.

Ինձ մեքենայի ապահովագրություն է պետք:

Indz mek'enayi apahovagrut'yun e petk'.

135 - 2

A roll of tissue.

Հյուսվածքի գլան:

Hyusvatsk'i glan:

135 - 3

He clenched his fists.

Նա սեղմեց բռունցքները:

Na seghmets' brrunts'k'nery.

20/52

135 - 4

Please do not litter.

Խնդրում եմ մի թափեք աղբը:

Khndrum yem mi t'ap'ek' aghby:

135 - 5

It's sunny.

Արև է:

Arev e.

135 - 6

I have no problem.

Ես խնդիր չունեմ:

Yes khndir ch'unem.

135 - 7

Her cheeks are all red.

Նրա այտերը բոլորը կարմիր են:

Nra aytery bolory karmir yen:

Day 135

Week 20

136 - 1

I sat down on the bench.

Ես նստեցի նստարանին:

Yes nstets'i nstaranin.

136 - 2

Thanks a lot.

Շատ շնորհակալություն.

Shat shnorhakalut'yun.

136 - 3

The door bell rang.

Դռան զանգը հնչեց:

Drran zangy hnch'ets'.

20/52

136 - 4

You look pale.

Դու գունատ տեսք ունես:

Du gunat tesk' unes.

136 - 5

Do the home work.

Կատարեք տնային աշխատանքը:

Katarek' tnayin ashkhatank'y.

136 - 6

Thanks for the tip.

Շնորհակալություն հուշման համար:

Shnorhakalut'yun hushman hamar:

136 - 7

This cat is a female.

Այս կատուն էգ է:

Ays katun eg e.

Day 136

Week 20

137 - 1

My hobby is reading.

Իմ հոբբին կարդալն է:

Im hobbin kardaln e.

137 - 2

She left a message.

Նա հաղորդագրություն է թողել.

Na haghordagrut'yun e t'voghel.

137 - 3

You've made my day.

Դուք դարձրեցիք իմ օրը:

Duk' dardzrets'ik' im ory:

137 - 4

He stood on the stage.

Նա կանգնեց բեմի վրա:

Na kangnets' bemi vra.

137 - 5

Calm down.

Հանգստացիր.

Hangstats'ir.

137 - 6

Are you Ok?

Լավ ես?

Lav yes?

137 - 7

Do not cross.

Մի հատեք:

Mi hatek':

Day 137

Week 20

138 - 1

Repeat after me.

Կրկնել ինձանից հետո.

Krknel indzanits' heto.

138 - 2

Please think carefully.

Խնդրում եմ ուշադիր մտածեք:

Khndrum yem ushadir mtatsek'.

138 - 3

Safety comes first.

Անվտանգությունն առաջին տեղում է:

Anvtangut'yunn arrajin teghum e:

138 - 4

Have you ever had a pet?

Դուք երբևէ ընտանի կենդանի ունեցե՞լ եք:

Duk' yerbeve yntani kendani unets'e'l yek':

138 - 5

I feel tired.

Ես հոգնած եմ զգում:

Yes hognats yem zgum.

138 - 6

I'm sure about it.

Ես համոզված եմ դրանում:

Yes hamozvats yem dranum.

138 - 7

She reacted well.

Նա լավ արձագանքեց.

Na lav ardzagank'ets'.

Day 138

Week 20

139 - 1

Wake him up.

Արթնացրեք նրան:

Art'nats'rek' nran:

139 - 2

I am friendly person.

Ես ընկերասեր մարդ եմ:

Yes ynkeraser mard yem.

139 - 3

It is very hot inside.

Ներսում շատ շոգ է:

Nersum shat shog e.

139 - 4

Stop chattering.

Դադարեցրեք շաղակրատելը:

Dadarets'rek' shaghakrately:

139 - 5

He has a weak stomach.

Նա թույլ ստամոքս ունի:

Na t'uyl stamok's uni.

139 - 6

My feel hurt.

Ես վիրավորված եմ:

Yes viravorvats yem:

139 - 7

A leaf of lettuce.

Հազարի մի տերեւ.

Hazari mi terev.

Day 139

Test 20

140 - 1

What brings you here?

140 - 2

It's sunny.

140 - 3

You look pale.

20/52

140 - 4

You've made my day.

140 - 5

Please think carefully.

140 - 6

Wake him up.

140 - 7

A leaf of lettuce.

Day 140

Week 21

141 - 1

I have my own business.

Ես ունեմ իմ սեփական բիզնեսը:

Yes unem im sep'akan biznesy.

141 - 2

Enjoy your meal!

Բարի ախորժակ!

Bari akhorzhak!

141 - 3

I feel sick today.

Այսոր ես հիվանդ եմ զգում:

Aysor yes hivand yem zgum:

21/52

141 - 4

Did you enjoy your meal?

Դուք վայելե՞լ եք ձեր ճաշը:

Duk' vayele"l yek' dzer chashy:

141 - 5

Just a moment please.

Մի պահ, խնդրում եմ.

Mi pah, khndrum yem.

141 - 6

It's a great shame.

Մեծ ամոթ է:

Mets amot' e.

141 - 7

He's not arrogant.

Նա մեծամիտ չէ:

Na metsamit ch'e:

Day 141

Week 21

142 - 1

Lastly, you.

Ի վերջո, դուք.

I verjo, duk'.

142 - 2

He's incapable.

Նա անկարող է:

Na ankarogh e:

142 - 3

Let's go to bed.

Եկեք գնանք քնելու:

Yekek' gnank' k'nelu:

142 - 4

I lost my key today.

Այսոր ես կորցրել եմ իմ բանալին:

Aysor yes korts'rel yem im banalin:

142 - 5

I'll put you through.

Ես քեզ կանցկացնեմ:

Yes k'ez kants'kats'nem.

142 - 6

How can I get there?

Ինչպես կարող եմ հասնել այնտեղ?

Inch'pes karogh yem hasnel ayntegh?

142 - 7

He plays the guitar.

Նա կիթառ է նվագում:

Na kit'arr e nvagum.

Day 142

Week 21

143 - 1

I pickup very fast.

Ես շատ արագ եմ վերցնում:

Yes shat arag yem verts'num:

143 - 2

A sprig of parsley.

Մի ճյուղ մաղադանոս:

Mi chyugh maghadanos.

143 - 3

You must be tired

Դուք պետք է հոգնած լինեք

Duk' petk' e hognats linek'

21/52

143 - 4

Are you John?

Դու Ջոնն ես

Du Jonn yes

143 - 5

Roses smell sweet.

Վարդերի հոտը քաղցր է:

Varderi hoty k'aghts'r e:

143 - 6

Could I have a receipt?

Կարո՞ղ եմ անդորրագիր ունենալ:

Karo°gh yem andorragir unenal:

143 - 7

He's growing a beard.

Նա մորուք է թողնում:

Na moruk' e t'voghnum:

Day 143

Week 21

144 - 1

I added my own thought.

Ես ավելացրեցի իմ սեփական միտքը.

Yes avelats'rets'i im sep'akan mitk'y.

144 - 2

I prefer rice to bread.

Ես նախընտրում եմ բրինձը հացից:

Yes nakhyntrum yem brindzy hats'its'.

144 - 3

He's wearing glasses.

Նա ակնոց է կրում:

Na aknots' e krum:

21/52

144 - 4

Are they your relatives?

Նրանք ձեր ազգականնե՞րն են:

Nrank' dzer azgakanne°rn yen.

144 - 5

He is driving too fast.

Նա շատ արագ է վարում:

Na shat arag e varum.

144 - 6

Please boil some water.

Խնդրում ենք մի քիչ ջուր եռացնել:

Khndrum yenk' mi k'ich' jur yerrats'nel.

144 - 7

I bought one book.

Ես գնեցի մեկ գիրք.

Yes gnets'i mek girk'.

Day 144

Week 21

145 - 1

It's not my fault.

Դա իմ մեղքը չէ:

Da im meghk'y ch'e:

145 - 2

Can I take any message?

Կարո՞ղ եմ որևէ հաղորդագրություն ընդունել:

Karo"gh yem voreve haghordagrut'yun yndunel:

145 - 3

I have lost my card.

Ես կորցրել եմ իմ քարտը.

Yes korts'rel yem im k'arty.

21/52

145 - 4

Are you married?

Դուք ամուսնացա՞ծ եք:

Duk' amusnats'a"ts yek'.

145 - 5

I owe you an apology.

Ես քեզ ներողություն եմ պարտական:

Yes k'ez neroghut'yun yem partakan.

145 - 6

Which one do you want?

ո՞ր մեկն ես ուզում:

Vo"r mekn yes uzum.

145 - 7

I do the paperwork.

Ես կատարում եմ թղթաբանությունը:

Yes katarum yem t'ght'abanut'yuny.

Day 145

Week 21

146 - 1

My boss gave me his car.

Իմ ղեկավարն ինձ տվեց իր մեքենան։

Im ghekavarn indz tvets' ir mek'enan.

146 - 2

Who do you go with?

Ո՞ւմ հետ ես գնում։

VO"wm het yes gnum:

146 - 3

I go by train.

Ես գնում եմ գնացքով։

Yes gnum yem gnats'k'ov.

21/52

146 - 4

The food smells good.

Սնունդը լավ հոտ է գալիս։

Snundy lav hot e galis:

146 - 5

He's short.

Նա ցածրահասակ է։

Na ts'atsrahasak e'

146 - 6

Settle down, please.

Հանգստացեք, խնդրում եմ։

Hangstats'ek', khndrum yem:

146 - 7

I'm very hungry.

Ես շատ սոված եմ.

Yes shat sovats yem.

Day 146

Test 21

147 - 1

It's a great shame.

147 - 2

I'll put you through.

147 - 3

Are you John?

21/52

147 - 4

He's wearing glasses.

147 - 5

Can I take any message?

147 - 6

My boss gave me his car.

147 - 7

I'm very hungry.

Day 147

Week 22

148 - 1

How do you do?

Ողջույն?

Voghjuyn?

148 - 2

I have a sore throat.

Ես կոկորդի ցավ ունեմ:

Yes kokordi ts'av unem.

148 - 3

I go by bus.

Ես գնում եմ ավտոբուսով:

Yes gnum yem avtobusov.

22/52

148 - 4

There is an accident.

Վթար է տեղի ունեցել.

Vt'ar e teghi unets'el.

148 - 5

When do you go to bed?

Ե՞րբ ես գնում քնելու:

Yo՞rh yes gnum k'nelu:

148 - 6

I do not feel well.

Ես լավ չեմ զգում.

Yes lav ch'em zgum.

148 - 7

That was close.

Մոտ էր.

Mot er.

Day 148

Week 22

149 - 1

Go and get dressed.

Գնա հագնվիր:

Gna hagnvir.

149 - 2

Let's try harder.

Եկեք ավելի շատ փորձենք:

Yekek' aveli shat p'vordzenk':

149 - 3

Here is your key.

Ահա ձեր բանալին:

Aha dzer banalin:

22/52

149 - 4

When is it?

Երբ է դա?

Yerb e da?

149 - 5

It's stifling hot.

Խեղդող շոգ է:

KHeghdogh shog e:

149 - 6

Time flies.

Ժամանակը թռչում է.

Zhamanaky t'rrch'um e.

149 - 7

My watch is stopped.

Ժամացույցս կանգ է առել:

Zhamats'uyts's kang e arrel.

Day 149

Week 22

150 - 1

I'm not available today.

Ես այսօր հասանելի չեմ:

Yes aysor hasaneli ch'em:

150 - 2

His room is very dirty.

Նրա սենյակը շատ կեղտոտ է:

Nra senyaky shat keghtot e.

150 - 3

This soup is very hot.

Այս ապուրը շատ տաք է:

Ays apury shat tak' e.

22/52

150 - 4

He hates evil.

Նա ատում է չարը:

Na atum e ch'ary:

150 - 5

I loathe ironing.

Ես զզվում եմ արդուկելուց:

Yes zzvum yom ərdukeluts'.

150 - 6

Hang on for a moment.

Մի պահ սպասիր:

Mi pah spasir.

150 - 7

The ship sank.

Նավը խորտակվեց:

Navy khortakvets'.

Day 150

Week 22

151 - 1

It's a pleasant morning.

Հաճելի առավոտ է:

Hacheli arravot e.

151 - 2

Certainly.

Անշուշտ:

Anshusht.

151 - 3

There's nothing here.

Այստեղ ոչինչ չկա:

Aystegh voch'inch' ch'ka:

22/52

151 - 4

This door is automatic.

Այս դուռը ավտոմատ է:

Ays durry avtomat e.

151 - 5

His story is boring.

Նրա պատմությունը ձանձրալի է:

Nra patmut'yuny dzandzrali e:

151 - 6

The exam was difficult.

Քննությունը դժվար էր.

K'nnut'yuny dzhvar er.

151 - 7

It's 16th June.

Հունիսի 16-ն է:

Hunisi 16-n e.

Day 151

Week 22

152 - 1

Where's the bathroom?

Որտեղ է լոգարանը?

Vortegh e logarany?

152 - 2

He left the group.

Նա դուրս եկավ խմբից:

Na durs yekav khmbits'.

152 - 3

He is smart.

Նա խելացի է:

Na khelats'i e.

22/52

152 - 4

I read the Times.

Ես կարդացել եմ Times-ը:

Yes kardats'el yem Times-y:

152 - 5

Your number please.

Ձեր համարը խնդրում եմ:

Dzer hamary khndrum yem.

152 - 6

I need to get a job.

Ինձ պետք է աշխատանք գտնել:

Indz petk' e ashkhatank' gtnel:

152 - 7

Wait for sometime.

Սպասեք որոշ ժամանակ:

Spasek' vorosh zhamanak:

Day 152

Week 22

153 - 1

He won the election.

Նա հաղթեց ընտրություններում:

Na haght'ets' yntrut'yunnerum.

153 - 2

Don't beat him.

Մի ծեծեք նրան:

Mi tsetsek' nran:

153 - 3

I need more exercise.

Ինձ ավելի շատ վարժություն է պետք:

Indz aveli shat varzhut'yun e petk':

153 - 4

Poor you.

Խե՜ղճ.

KHe¯ghch.

153 - 5

What is your dream job?

Որն է քո երազանքի աշխատանքը?

Vorn e k'vo yerazank'i ashkhatank'y?

153 - 6

Please do.

Խնդրում եմ անել:

Khndrum yem anel:

153 - 7

I am so into you.

Ես այնքան եմ քո հանդեպ:

Yes aynk'an yem k'vo handep:

Day 153

Test 22

154 - 1

I do not feel well.

154 - 2

It's stifling hot.

154 - 3

He hates evil.

22/52

154 - 4

There's nothing here.

154 - 5

He left the group.

154 - 6

He won the election.

154 - 7

I am so into you.

Day 154

Week 23

155 - 1

I like French food.

Ես սիրում եմ ֆրանսիական սնունդ:

Yes sirum yem fransiakan snund:

155 - 2

Fasten your seat belt.

Ամրացնել ձեր ամրագոտիները.

Amrats'nel dzer amragotinery.

155 - 3

This is a true story.

Սա իրական պատմություն է:

Sa irakan patmut'yun e.

23/52

155 - 4

I'm hungry.

Ես սոված եմ.

Yes sovats yem.

155 - 5

Both are the same.

Երկուսն էլ նույնն են:

Yerkusn el nuynn yen.

155 - 6

He believes in God.

Նա հավատում է Աստծուն:

Na havatum e Asttsun:

155 - 7

This is my house.

Սա է իմ տունը.

Sa e im tuny.

Day 155

Week 23

156 - 1

This is my friend.

Սա իմ ընկերն է.

Sa im ynkern e.

156 - 2

I have a bad cold.

Ես վատ մրսում եմ:

Yes vat mrsum yem.

156 - 3

She's always smiling.

Նա միշտ ժպտում է:

Na misht zhptum e:

156 - 4

Please go in front.

Խնդրում եմ, գնացեք առջև:

Khndrum yem, gnats'ek' arrjev:

156 - 5

Next please.

Հաջորդը խնդրում եմ:

Hajordy khndrum yem.

156 - 6

You don't have to wait.

Պետք չէ սպասել:

Petk' ch'e spasel:

156 - 7

Never mind.

Դեմ չէ:

Dem ch'e:

Day 156

Week 23

157 - 1

She talks a lot.

Նա շատ է խոսում:

Na shat e khosum:

157 - 2

I'm frightened.

Ես վախեցած եմ:

Yes vakhets'ats yem.

157 - 3

I am on a diet.

Ես դիետայի վրա եմ:

Yes diyetayi vra yem.

23/52

157 - 4

I'm grilling fish now.

Ես հիմա ձուկ եմ խորովում:

Yes hima dzuk yem khorovum:

157 - 5

Did you get my letter?

Ստացա՞ք իմ նամակը:

Stats'a˝k' im namaky.

157 - 6

She's in the movie.

Նա ֆիլմում է:

Na filmum e:

157 - 7

I'm feeling better.

Ես ինձ ավելի լավ եմ զգում:

Yes indz aveli lav yem zgum:

Day 157

Week 23

158 - 1

Can I leave a message?

Կարո՞դ եմ հաղորդագրություն թողնել։

Karo°gh yem haghordagrut'yun t'voghnel:

158 - 2

I have got a puncture.

Ես պունկցիա եմ ստացել։

Yes punkts'ia yem stats'el.

158 - 3

Happy New Year!

Շնորհավոր Նոր Տարի!

Shnorhavor Nor Tari!

158 - 4

23/52

The water has boiled.

Ջուրը եռացել է։

Jury yerrats'el e.

158 - 5

Do some yoga.

Մի քիչ յոգա արեք։

Mi k'ich' yoga nrek'.

158 - 6

No problem.

Ոչ մի խնդիր.

Voch' mi khndir.

158 - 7

I'll be online.

Ես կլինեմ առցանց։

Yes klinem arrts'ants':

Day 158

Week 23

159 - 1

I need health insurance.

Ինձ պետք է առողջության ապահովագրություն:

Indz petk' e arroghjut'yan apahovagrut'yun:

159 - 2

Let's ask Mom.

Եկեք հարցնենք մայրիկին.

Yekek' harts'nenk' mayrikin.

159 - 3

He got the silver medal.

Նա ստացել է արծաթե մեդալ:

Na stats'el e artsat'e medal.

23/52

159 - 4

I read your book.

Ես կարդացի քո գիրքը:

Yes kardats'i k'vo girk'y:

159 - 5

Are you good at tennis?

Դուք լավ եք թենիսում:

Duk' lav yek' t'enisum:

159 - 6

Leave me alone.

Ինձ մենակ թող.

Indz menak t'vogh.

159 - 7

Do you have any idea?

Դուք գաղափար ունե՞ք:

Duk' gaghap'ar une"k'.

Day 159

Week 23

160 - 1

I really appreciate it.

Ես իսկապես գնահատում եմ դա:

Yes iskapes gnahatum yem da:

160 - 2

Get out of my sight.

Հեռացիր իմ աչքից:

Herrats'ir im ach'k'its'.

160 - 3

He's a wonderful man.

Նա հիանալի մարդ է:

Na hianali mard e:

23/52

160 - 4

You can't.

Չես կարող:

CH'es karogh.

160 - 5

The dog bit my hand.

Շունը կծեց ձեռքս:

Shuny ktnnt'ə' dxeıı k'ʮ.

160 - 6

Did you return the book?

Գիրքը վերադարձրե՞լ եք:

Girk'y veradardzre°l yek'.

160 - 7

I am a computer analyst.

Ես համակարգչային վերլուծաբան եմ:

Yes hamakargch'ayin verlutsaban yem.

Day 160

Test 23

161 - 1

He believes in God.

161 - 2

Next please.

161 - 3

I'm grilling fish now.

23/52

161 - 4

Happy New Year!

161 - 5

Let's ask Mom.

161 - 6

I really appreciate it.

161 - 7

I am a computer analyst.

Day 161

Week 24

162 - 1

He was sent to England.
Նրան ուղարկեցին Անգլիա:
Nran ugharkets'in Anglia.

162 - 2

This dish is delicious.
Այս ուտեստը համեղ է:
Ays utesty hamegh e.

162 - 3

It is not your fault.
Դա քո մեղքը չէ:
Da k'vo meghk'y ch'e.

162 - 4

24/52

How's your day going?
Ինչպես է անցնում քո օրը?
Inch'pes e ants'num k'vo ory?

162 - 5

I just love to travel.
Ես պարզապես սիրում եմ ճանապարհորդել:
Yes parzapes sirum yem chanaparhordel:

162 - 6

Sure, I'd be glad to.
Իհարկե, ես ուրախ կլինեմ:
Iharke, yes urakh klinem:

162 - 7

My son broke my glasses.
Տղաս կոտրեց ակնոցս.
Tghas kotrets' aknots's.

Day 162

Week 24

163 - 1

Have a walk.

Զբոսնեք:

Zbosnek'.

163 - 2

Do you want a receipt?

Ուզու°մ եք անդորրագիր:

Uzu"m yek' andorragir.

163 - 3

I caught a butterfly.

Ես թիթեռ եմ բռնել:

Yes t'it'err yem brrnel.

24/52

163 - 4

No thanks, I'll pass.

Ոչ, շնորհակալություն, ես կանցնեմ:

Voch', shnorhakalut'yun, yes kants'nem:

163 - 5

I will consult my boss.

Ես կխորհրդակցեմ իմ ղեկավարի հետ:

Yes kkhorhrdakts'em im ghekavari het:

163 - 6

It's my duty to do it.

Իմ պարտքն է դա անել:

Im partk'n e da anel:

163 - 7

I think it's boring.

Կարծում եմ, որ դա ձանձրալի է:

Kartsum yem, vor da dzandzrali e:

Day 163

Week 24

164 - 1

Who am I talking to?

Ո՞ւմ հետ եմ խոսում:

VO"wm het yem khosum.

164 - 2

A stick of butter.

Մի ձողիկ կարագ:

Mi dzoghik karag.

164 - 3

The house is lovely.

Տունը սիրուն է:

Tuny sirun e.

164 - 4

A tube of toothpaste.

Ատամի մածուկի խողովակ:

Atami matsuki khoghovak:

24/52

164 - 5

One of my eyes is itchy.

Աչքերիցս մեկը քոր է գալիս:

Ach'k'erits'n meky k'vor e gulls.

164 - 6

My kid wants some juice.

Իմ երեխան մի քիչ հյութ է ուզում:

Im yerekhan mi k'ich' hyut' e uzum:

164 - 7

My luggage is lost.

Իմ ուղեբերը կորել է:

Im ugheberry korel e.

Day 164

Week 24

165 - 1

I drank a little wine.

Ես մի քիչ գինի խմեցի:

Yes mi k'ich' gini khmets'i.

165 - 2

Here's thirty dollars.

Ահա երեսուն դոլար:

Aha yeresun dolar:

165 - 3

She's an office worker.

Նա գրասենյակի աշխատող է:

Na grasenyaki ashkhatogh e:

24/52

165 - 4

May I have a word?

Կարո՞ղ եմ խոսք ասել:

Karo°gh yem khosk' asel:

165 - 5

He's surely a hero.

Նա, անշուշտ, հերոս է:

Na, anshusht, heros e:

165 - 6

Good night.

Բարի գիշեր.

Bari gisher.

165 - 7

My car has broken down.

Իմ մեքենան փչացել է.

Im mek'enan p'ch'ats'el e.

Day 165

Week 24

166 - 1

How was your vacation?

Ինչպե՞ս անցավ ձեր արձակուրդը:

Inch'pe"s ants'av dzer ardzakurdy:

166 - 2

It's cold.

Ցուրտ է:

Ts'urt e.

166 - 3

I want to disappear now.

Ես հիմա ուզում եմ անհետանալ:

Yes hima uzum yem anhetanal.

166 - 4

What can I do for you?

Ինչ կարող եմ անել քեզ համար?

Inch' karogh yem anel k'ez hamar?

24/52

166 - 5

My watch is slow.

Իմ ժամացույցը դանդաղ է:

Im zhamats'uyts'y dandagh e.

166 - 6

I forgot my handbag.

Ես մոռացել եմ իմ ձերքի պայուսակը.

Yes morrats'el yem im dzerrk'i payusaky.

166 - 7

Whose parcel is this?

Ո՞ւմ ծանրոցն է սա:

VO"wm tsanrots'n e sa:

Day 166

Week 24

167 - 1

My wife is from London.

Կինս Լոնդոնից է:

Kins Londonits' e.

167 - 2

Her face is pale.

Նրա դեմքը գունատ է:

Nra demk'y gunat e.

167 - 3

He has my number.

Նա ունի իմ համարը:

Na uni im hamary.

24/52

167 - 4

I will call you later.

Ես քեզ ավելի ուշ կզանգեմ:

Yes k'ez aveli ush kzangem.

167 - 5

What are you doing?

Ի՞նչ ես անում?

Inch' yes anum?

167 - 6

Switch off the T.V.

Անջատեք հեռուստացույցը

Anjatek' herrustats'uyts'y

167 - 7

I love animals.

Ես սիրում եմ կենդանիներին.

Yes sirum yem kendaninerin.

Day 167

Test 24

168 - 1

Sure, I'd be glad to.

168 - 2

I will consult my boss.

168 - 3

A tube of toothpaste.

168 - 4

She's an office worker.

24/52

168 - 5

It's cold.

168 - 6

My wife is from London.

168 - 7

I love animals.

Day 168

Week 25

169 - 1

He lost consciousness.

Նա կորցրել է գիտակցությունը:

Na korts'rel e gitakts'ut'yuny.

169 - 2

I have no other choice.

Ես այլ ելք չունեմ:

Yes ayl yelk' ch'unem.

169 - 3

The time now is 6:35.

Ժամն այժմ 6:35 է:

Zhamn ayzhm 6:35 e:

25/52

169 - 4

I am from Paris.

Ես Փարիզից եմ:

Yes P'arizits' yem.

169 - 5

I'm angry about.

Ես բարկանում եմ.

Yes barkanum yem.

169 - 6

The line is busy.

Գիծը զբաղված է:

Gitsy zbaghvats e.

169 - 7

My boss is stubborn.

Իմ ղեկավարը համառ է.

Im ghekavary hamarr e.

Day 169

Week 25

170 - 1

Where do you work?

Որտեղ ես դու աշխատում?

Vortegh yes du ashkhatum?

170 - 2

This river is shallow.

Այս գետը ծանծաղ է:

Ays gety tsantsagh e.

170 - 3

I'd love to, thanks.

Ես կցանկանայի, շնորհակալություն:

Yes kts'ankanayi, shnorhakalut'yun:

170 - 4

Listen to your body.

Լսեք ձեր մարմնին.

Lsek' dzer marmnin.

25/52

170 - 5

I am sorry to hear that.

Ցավում եմ դա լսելու համար:

Ts'avum yem da lselu humar.

170 - 6

He felt miserable.

Նա իրեն դժբախտ էր զգում:

Na iren dzhbakht er zgum.

170 - 7

My palms are sweaty.

Ափերս քրտնած են:

Ap'ers k'rtnats yen.

Day 170

Week 25

171 - 1

Can you drive a truck?

Կարո՞ղ եք բեռնատար վարել:

Karo°gh yek' berrnatar varel:

171 - 2

How do you know her?

Ինչպե՞ս եք ճանաչում նրան:

Inch'pe°s yek' chanach'um nran:

171 - 3

Thanks.

Շնորհակալություն:

Shnorhakalut'yun.

171 - 4

25/52

It's ten past eleven.

Ժամը տասնմեկ անց տասն է:

Zhamy tasnmek ants' tasn e.

171 - 5

You are beautiful.

Դու գեղեցիկ ես.

Du geghets'ik yes.

171 - 6

Did I ask you?

Ես քեզ հարցրի՞ր:

Yes k'ez harts'ri°r.

171 - 7

It hurts.

Ցավեցնում է.

Ts'avets'num e.

Day 171

Week 25

172 - 1

Where is the post box?

Որտեղ է փոստային արկղը:

Vortegh e p'vostayin arkghy:

172 - 2

Welcome to Japan.

Բարի գալուստ Ճապոնիա:

Bari galust Chaponia.

172 - 3

I like grapes.

Ես սիրում եմ խաղող:

Yes sirum yem khaghogh:

172 - 4

I will try this.

Ես կփորձեմ սա:

Yes kp'vordzem sa:

25/52

172 - 5

I hate tests.

Ես ատում եմ թեստերը:

Yes atum yem t'esteiy.

172 - 6

Are you free tomorrow?

Վաղը ազատ եք?

Vaghy azat yek'?

172 - 7

My shoulders are stiff.

Ուսերս կոշտացել են:

Users koshtats'el yen.

Day 172

Week 25

173 - 1

May I take your order?

Կարո՞ղ եմ վերցնել ձեր պատվերը:

Karo°gh yem verts'nel dzer patvery:

173 - 2

Sorry. You can't.

Ներողություն. Չես կարող:

Neroghut'yun. CH'es karogh.

173 - 3

What did he ask you?

Ի՞նչ հարցրեց նա քեզ:

I°nch' harts'rets' na k'ez:

173 - 4

25/52

I'm from the U.S.

Ես ԱՄՆ-ից եմ

Yes AMN-its' yem

173 - 5

He has a clean image.

Նա մաքուր կերպար ունի:

Na mak'ur kerpar uni.

173 - 6

I like your haircut.

Ինձ դուր է գալիս քո սանրվածքը:

Indz dur e galis k'vo sanrvatsk'y:

173 - 7

It looks great!

Այն հիանալի տեսք ունի:

Ayn hianali tesk' uni:

Day 173

Week 25

174 - 1

When is he expected?

Ե՞րբ է նրան սպասվում:

Ye°rb e nran spasvum:

174 - 2

Don't be late.

Մի ուշացեք.

Mi ushats'ek'.

174 - 3

He laughed loudly.

Նա բարձր ծիծաղեց:

Na bardzr tsitsaghets'.

174 - 4

Are you going with them?

Դուք գնում եք նրանց հետ?

Duk' gnum yek' nrants' het?

25/52

174 - 5

It's yummy.

Համեղ է:

Hamegh e:

174 - 6

The rain stopped.

Անձրևը դադարեց:

Andzrevy dadarets'.

174 - 7

Do not lose your ticket.

Մի կորցրեք ձեր տոմսը:

Mi korts'rek' dzer tomsy:

Day 174

Test 25

175 - 1

The line is busy.

175 - 2

I am sorry to hear that.

175 - 3

It's ten past eleven.

175 - 4

I like grapes.

25/52

175 - 5

Sorry. You can't.

175 - 6

When is he expected?

175 - 7

Do not lose your ticket.

Day 175

Week 26

176 - 1

Solve the equation.

Լուծե՛ք հավասարումը.

Lutse'k' havasarumy.

176 - 2

Perfect!

Կատարյալ!

Kataryal!

176 - 3

I fed the dog.

Ես կերակրեցի շանը:

Yes kerakrets'i shany:

176 - 4

She's a romantic person.

Նա ռոմանտիկ մարդ է:

Na rromantik mard e:

26/52

176 - 5

That's not right.

Դա ճիշտ չէ.

Da chinht ch'e.

176 - 6

How much should I pay?

Որքա՞ն պետք է վճարեմ:

Vork'a°n petk' e vcharem:

176 - 7

It's time to leave.

Ժամանակն է հեռանալ:

Zhamanakn e herranal.

Day 176

Week 26

177 - 1

Can I borrow a pen?

Կարո՞ղ եմ գրիչ վերցնել:

Karo°gh yem grich' verts'nel:

177 - 2

He threw the ball.

Նա նետեց գնդակը:

Na netets' gndaky.

177 - 3

Please open to page 32.

Խնդրում ենք բացել էջ 32:

Khndrum yenk' bats'el ej 32.

26/52

177 - 4

I'm very sleepy today.

Ես այսոր շատ քնկոտ եմ:

Yes aysor shat k'nkot yem:

177 - 5

The train is crowded.

Գնացքը մարդաշատ է:

Gnats'k'y mardashat e.

177 - 6

I love tomatoes.

Ես սիրում եմ լոլիկ.

Yes sirum yem lolik.

177 - 7

Do you think so?

Դուք այդպես եք կարծում:

Duk' aydpes yek' kartsum:

Day 177

Week 26

178 - 1

Do you do alterations?

Փոփոխություններ անո°ւմ եք:

P'vop'vokhut'yunner ano°wm yek'.

178 - 2

Bye for now.

Առայժմ.

Arrayzhm.

178 - 3

I'm painting the wall.

Ես նկարում եմ պատը:

Yes nkarum yem paty:

178 - 4

Please give me a hint.

Խնդրում եմ ինձ մի հուշում տվեք:

Khndrum yem indz mi hushum tvek':

26/52

178 - 5

Nice wearther, isn't it?

Հաձելի է հագնվել, այնպես չէ°:

Hacheli e hagnvel, aynpes ch'e°.

178 - 6

I keep my promise.

Ես պահում եմ իմ խոստումը.

Yes pahum yem im khostumy.

178 - 7

My boss is very strict.

Իմ ղեկավարը շատ խիստ է.

Im ghekavary shat khist e.

Day 178

Week 26

179 - 1

Please keep working.

Խնդրում եմ շարունակեք աշխատել:

Khndrum yem sharunakek' ashkhatel.

179 - 2

I found a new job.

Նոր աշխատանք գտա.

Nor ashkhatank' gta.

179 - 3

The diamond glittered.

Ադամանդը փայլեց:

Adamandy p'aylets'.

26/52

179 - 4

The man stole her bag.

Տղամարդը գողացել է նրա պայուսակը.

Tghamardy goghats'el e nra payusaky.

179 - 5

Good afternoon, Mrs.

Բարի օր, տիկին.

Bari or, tikin.

179 - 6

Let's keep in touch!

Եկ կապի մեջ մնանք!

Yek kapi mej mnank'!

179 - 7

It wasn't me.

Ես չէի:

Yes ch'ei.

Day 179

Week 26

180 - 1

Yes, you can.

Այո, դու կարող ես.

Ayo, du karogh yes.

180 - 2

He has a car.

Նա մեքենա ունի:

Na mek'ena uni.

180 - 3

You need to swipe it.

Դուք պետք է սահեցնեք այն:

Duk' petk' e sahets'nek' ayn:

180 - 4

I don't watch much TV.

Ես շատ հեռուստացույց չեմ դիտում:

Yes shat herrustats'uyts' ch'em ditum:

26/52

180 - 5

I'm afraid not.

Վախենում եմ՝ ոչ:

Vakhenum yem՝ voch'.

180 - 6

We are hungry.

Մենք քաղցած ենք.

Menk' k'aghts'ats yenk'.

180 - 7

The bus is leaving.

Ավտոբուսը մեկնում է:

Avtobusy meknum e.

Day 180

Week 26

181 - 1

They often play tennis.

Նրանք հաճախ թենիս են խաղում:

Nrank' hachakh t'enis yen khaghum.

181 - 2

Why do you suspect me?

Ինչո՞ւ ես ինձ կասկածում:

Inch'vo°w yes indz kaskatsum.

181 - 3

I swam a lot yesterday.

Երեկ ես շատ եմ լողացել:

Yerek yes shat yem loghats'el.

181 - 4

What's your question?

Ո՞րն է ձեր հարցը:

VO°rn e dzer harts'y:

181 - 5

I like bitter coffee.

Ես սիրում եմ դառը սուրճ:

Yes sirum yem darry surch:

181 - 6

I love you.

Ես քեզ սիրում եմ.

Yes k'ez sirum yem.

181 - 7

He gulped down water.

Նա ջուրը կուլ տվեց:

Na jury kul tvets'.

Day 181

Test 26

182 - 1

How much should I pay?

182 - 2

The train is crowded.

182 - 3

Please give me a hint.

182 - 4

The diamond glittered.

26/52

182 - 5

He has a car.

182 - 6

They often play tennis.

182 - 7

He gulped down water.

Day 182

Week 27

183 - 1

I want more freedom.

Ես ավելի շատ ազատություն եմ ուզում:

Yes aveli shat azatut'yun yem uzum.

183 - 2

There's a bomb!

Ռումբ կա:

Rrumb ka.

183 - 3

I go by cycle.

Ես գնում եմ ցիկլով:

Yes gnum yem ts'iklov:

183 - 4

Mind your tongue.

Ուշադրություն դարձրեք ձեր լեզվին:

Ushadrut'yun dardzrek' dzer lezvin:

27/52

183 - 5

Good job.

Լավ աշխատանք.

Lav ashkhatank'.

183 - 6

How was your day?

Ինչպես անցավ օրդ?

Inch'pes ants'av ord?

183 - 7

Think nothing of it.

Մի մտածիր դրա մասին:

Mi mtatsir dra masin:

Day 183

Week 27

184 - 1

He always wears jeans.

Նա միշտ ջինս է հագնում:

Na misht jins e hagnum.

184 - 2

Meet them in person.

Անձամբ հանդիպեք նրանց:

Andzamb handipek' nrants':

184 - 3

Who told you?

Ով քեզ ասաց?

Ov k'ez asats'?

184 - 4

I miss you.

Ես կարոտում ձեզ.

Yes karotum dzez.

27/52

184 - 5

She smiled at me.

Նա ժպտաց ինձ:

Na zhptats' indz:

184 - 6

What a pity.

Ինչ ափսոս.

Inch' ap'sos.

184 - 7

Can I use the gym?

Կարո՞ղ եմ օգտվել մարզասրահից:

Karo°gh yem ogtvel marzasrahits':

Day 184

Week 27

185 - 1

Hold the line, please.

Պահպանե՛ք տողը, խնդրում եմ:

Pahpane'k' toghy, khndrum yem:

185 - 2

I slept well last night.

Երեկ գիշեր լավ քնեցի:

Yerek gisher lav k'nets'i.

185 - 3

It's pay day!

Վճարման օր է:

Vcharman or e.

185 - 4

I have a stomach ache.

Ես ստամոքսի ցավ ունեմ:

Yes stamok'si ts'av unem.

185 - 5

That movie was boring.

Այդ ֆիլմը ձանձրալի էր:

Ayd filmy dzandzrali er.

185 - 6

A pack of vitamins.

Վիտամինների փաթեթ.

Vitaminneri p'at'et'.

185 - 7

I love my job.

Ես սիրում եմ իմ աշխատանքը.

Yes sirum yem im ashkhatank'y.

Day 185

Week 27

186 - 1

I didn't order that.

Ես դա չեմ պատվիրել:

Yes da ch'em patvirel:

186 - 2

No one knows the future.

Ոչ ոք չգիտի ապագան:

Voch' vok' ch'giti apagan:

186 - 3

Emergency telephone.

Շտապ հեռախոս.

Shtap herrakhos.

186 - 4

Smoking area.

Ծխելու տարածք.

Tskhelu taratsk'.

27/52

186 - 5

Good morning, teacher.

Բարի առավոտ ուսուցիչ.

Bari arravot usuts'ich'.

186 - 6

Don't threaten me.

Ինձ մի սպառնա:

Indz mi sparrna:

186 - 7

What's your view?

Ի՞նչ տեսակետ ունեք:

I˚nch' tesaket unek':

Day 186

Week 27

187 - 1

He's older than me.

Նա ինձնից մեծ է:

Na indznits' mets e:

187 - 2

I love to eat.

Ես սիրում եմ ուտել.

Yes sirum yem utel.

187 - 3

Shall we start?

Սկսե՞նք:

Skse"nk'.

187 - 4

She wore a purple dress.

Նա կրում էր մանուշակագույն զգեստ:

Na krum er manushakaguyn zgest.

27/52

187 - 5

She has thick eyebrows.

Նա հաստ հոնքեր ունի:

Na hast honk'er uni:

187 - 6

We had a smooth landing.

Մենք սահուն վայրէջք ունեցանք:

Menk' sahun vayrejk' unets'ank'.

187 - 7

Have a good time.

Լավ ժամանակ անցկացրու.

Lav zhamanak ants'kats'ru.

Day 187

Week 27

188 - 1

When is he returning?

Ե՞րբ է նա վերադառնում:

Ye°rb e na veradarrnum:

188 - 2

Which is your bag?

Ո՞րն է քո պայուսակը:

VO°rn e k'vo payusaky:

188 - 3

I had cake for dessert.

Ես աղանդերի համար տորթ ունեի:

Yes aghanderi hamar tort' unev:

188 - 4

Give me a life vest.

Տուր ինձ փրկարար բաճկոն:

Tur indz p'rkarar bachkon:

27/52

188 - 5

I am so sorry.

Ես իսկապես ցավում եմ.

Yes iskapes ts'avum yem.

188 - 6

I hate to tell you but.

Ես ատում եմ ձեզ ասել, բայց.

Yes atum yem dzez asel, bayts'.

188 - 7

That's what I think too.

Ես նույնպես այդպես եմ մտածում:

Yes nuynpes aydpes yem mtatsum.

Day 188

Test 27

189 - 1

How was your day?

189 - 2

She smiled at me.

189 - 3

I have a stomach ache.

189 - 4

Emergency telephone.

27/52

189 - 5

I love to eat.

189 - 6

When is he returning?

189 - 7

That's what I think too.

Day 189

Week 28

190 - 1

Bless you!

Առողջություն!

Arroghjut'yun!

190 - 2

Are you aware of that?

Դուք տեղյա°կ եք այդ մասին:

Duk' teghya°k yek' ayd masin.

190 - 3

Do you have insurance?

Դուք ապահովագրություն ունե°ք:

Duk' apahovagrut'yun une°k'.

190 - 4

I arrived home safely.

Ես ապահով հասա տուն:

Yes apahov hasa tun.

28/52

190 - 5

It's a full moon today.

Այսոր լիալուսին է:

Aysor lialusin e.

190 - 6

What a stubborn child!

Ի°նչ համառ երեխա է:

I°nch' hamarr yerekha e.

190 - 7

I'm working as a waiter.

Ես մատուցող եմ աշխատում:

Yes matuts'vogh yem ashkhatum.

Day 190

Week 28

191 - 1

Very Good!

Շատ լավ!

Shat lav!

191 - 2

She's 27 years old.

Նա 27 տարեկան է:

Na 27 tarekan e.

191 - 3

This is my fiancé.

Սա իմ նշանածն է:

Sa im nshanatsn e.

191 - 4

He took a deep breath.

Նա խորը շունչ քաշեց:

Na khory shunch' k'ashets'.

28/52

191 - 5

Insert card here.

Տեղադրեք քարտը այստեղ:

Teghadrek' k'arty aystegh:

191 - 6

Keep the change.

Պահել փոփոխությունը.

Pahel p'vop'vokhut'yuny.

191 - 7

I decided to marry her.

Ես որոշեցի ամուսնանալ նրա հետ:

Yes voroshets'i amusnanal nra het.

Day 191

Week 28

192 - 1

Boys, be ambitious.

Տղաներ, ամբիցիոզ եղեք:

Tghaner, ambits'ioz yeghek'.

192 - 2

Well done.

Լավ արեցիք:

Lav arets'ik'.

192 - 3

It's warm.

Տաք է:

Tak' e.

192 - 4

Life in Spain is fun.

Իսպանիայում կյանքը զվարճալի է.

Ispaniayum kyank'y zvarchali e.

28/52

192 - 5

I'm positive.

Ես դրական եմ տրամադրված:

Yoo drakan yem tramadrvats:

192 - 6

Where is his residence?

Որտեղ է նրա նստավայրը:

Vortegh e nra nstavayry:

192 - 7

Is John in?

Ջոնը մե՞ջ է:

Jony me¨j e:

Day 192

Week 28

193 - 1

It's too short.

Դա չափազանց կարճ է:

Da ch'ap'azants' karch e:

193 - 2

What a nice apartment.

Ինչ լավ բնակարան է:

Inch' lav bnakaran e:

193 - 3

I have no objection.

Ես առարկություն չունեմ:

Yes arrarkut'yun ch'unem.

193 - 4

The movie opens today.

Ֆիլմը բացվում է այսոր:

Filmy bats'vum e aysor.

28/52

193 - 5

Gentle wet cleaning.

Նուրբ թաց մաքրում:

Nurb t'ats' mak'rum.

193 - 6

The floor is slippery.

Հատակը սայթաքուն է:

Hataky sayt'ak'un e.

193 - 7

What day is it?

Ինչ օր է դա?

Inch' or e da?

Day 193

Week 28

194 - 1

How disappointing.

Որքան հիասթափեցնող:

Vork'an hiast'ap'ets'nogh:

194 - 2

Turn left.

Թեքվեք ձախ:

T'ek'vek' dzakh:

194 - 3

Please include me.

Խնդրում եմ ներառեք ինձ:

Khndrum yem nerarrek' indz:

194 - 4

Stop the car.

Կանգնեցրեք մեքենան:

Kangnets'rek' mek'enan.

194 - 5

Yes, I'd love too.

Այո, ես նույնպես կցանկանայի:

Ayo, yes nuynpes kts'ankanayi:

194 - 6

I remembered the past.

Ես հիշեցի անցյալը.

Yes hishets'i ants'yaly.

194 - 7

I know that.

Ես դա գիտեմ.

Yes da gitem.

Day 194

Week 28

195 - 1

That's a nuisance.

Դա անհանգստություն է:

Da anhangstut'yun e:

195 - 2

I'm learning judo.

Ես ձյուդո եմ սովորում:

Yes dzyudo yem sovorum:

195 - 3

It rained yesterday.

Երեկ անձրև եկավ:

Yerek andzrev yekav.

195 - 4

I feel chilly somehow.

Ինչ-որ կերպ ցուրտ եմ զգում:

Inch'-vor kerp ts'urt yem zgum:

28/52

195 - 5

Is the shop open?

Խանութը բացվա՞ծ է:

Khanut'y bats'va"ts e.

195 - 6

What time is it leaving?

Ժամը քանիսն է մեկնում:

Zhamy k'anisn e meknum:

195 - 7

A spoonful of honey.

Մի գդալ մեղր:

Mi gdal meghr.

Day 195

Test 28

196 - 1

What a stubborn child!

196 - 2

Insert card here.

196 - 3

Life in Spain is fun.

196 - 4

I have no objection.

28/52

196 - 5

Turn left.

196 - 6

That's a nuisance.

196 - 7

A spoonful of honey.

Day 196

Week 29

197 - 1

How can I help you?

Ինչպես կարող եմ օգնել քեզ?

Inch'pes karogh yem ognel k'ez?

197 - 2

That's great.

Դա հիանալի է:

Da hianali e:

197 - 3

Please keep quiet.

Խնդրում եմ լռեք:

Khndrum yem lrrek'.

197 - 4

Don't get angry.

Մի բարկացիր:

Mi barkats'ir.

29/52

197 - 5

Turn around.

Շրջվել.

Shrjvel.

197 - 6

My shoes got dirty.

Կոշիկս կեղտոտվեց:

Koshiks keghtotvets'.

197 - 7

That sounds nice.

Լավ է հնչում.

Lav e hnch'um.

Day 197

Week 29

198 - 1

It's too small for me.

Դա շատ փոքր է ինձ համար:

Da shat p'vok'r e indz hamar:

198 - 2

It smells good.

Լավ հոտ է գալիս:

Lav hot e galis:

198 - 3

I have a fever.

Ես ջերմություն ունեմ:

Yes jermut'yun unem.

198 - 4

Thanks so much.

Շատ շնորհակալություն.

Shat shnorhakalut'yun.

29/52

198 - 5

It is as you say.

Դա այնպես է, ինչպես ասում եք.

Da aynpon e, inch'pes asum yek'.

198 - 6

I live with my friends.

Ես ապրում եմ իմ ընկերների հետ:

Yes aprum yem im ynkerneri het.

198 - 7

I have an idea.

Ես մի գաղափար ունեմ.

Yes mi gaghap'ar unem.

Day 198

Week 29

199 - 1

That's fine.

Դա լավ է:

Da lav e:

199 - 2

You couldn't do that.

Դուք չէիք կարող դա անել:

Duk' ch'eik' karogh da anel:

199 - 3

This is my brother.

Սա իմ եղբայրն է:

Sa im yeghbayrn e.

199 - 4

I bought three glasses.

Ես գնել եմ երեք բաժակ:

Yes gnel yem yerek' bazhak:

29/52

199 - 5

Where are you now?

Որտեղ ես հիմա?

Vortegh yes hima?

199 - 6

You should read a lot.

Պետք է շատ կարդալ:

Petk' e shat kardal.

199 - 7

Any ideas?

Կա՞ն գաղափարներ:

Ka˜n gaghap'arner:

Day 199

Week 29

200 - 1

How is everyone?

Ինչպես են բոլորը:

Inch'pes yen bolory:

200 - 2

The deadline is near.

Ժամկետը մոտ է:

Zhamkety mot e.

200 - 3

I don't have time now.

Ես հիմա ժամանակ չունեմ:

Yes hima zhamanak ch'unem:

200 - 4

Thunder is rumbling.

Որոտը դղրդում է:

Voroty dghrdum e.

29/52

200 - 5

He tested the software.

Նա փորձարկեց ծրագրակազմը:

Na p'vordzarketo' tnrngrakazmy.

200 - 6

Which one of these?

Սրանցից ո՞ր մեկը:

Srants'its' vo°r meky.

200 - 7

It's worth the price.

Դա արժե այն գինը:

Da arzhe ayn giny:

Day 200

Week 29

201 - 1

I don't like crowds.

Ես չեմ սիրում ամբոխը։

Yes ch'em sirum ambokhy:

201 - 2

I'm starving.

Ես սովամահ եմ լինում։

Yes sovamah yem linum.

201 - 3

I was busy this evening.

Այս երեկո ես զբաղված էի։

Ays yereko yes zbaghvats ei.

201 - 4

Yes. I have.

Այո՛։ Ես ունեմ.

Ayo'. Yes unem.

29/52

201 - 5

The bag was sold out.

Պայուսակը սպառված էր։

Payusaky sparrvats er.

201 - 6

I belong to New York.

Ես պատկանում եմ Նյու Յորքին։

Yes patkanum yem Nyu York'in.

201 - 7

I don't mind it at all.

Ես ընդհանրապես դեմ չեմ։

Yes yndhanrapes dem ch'em:

Day 201

Week 29

202 - 1

I'll go there by train.
Ես այնտեղ կգնամ գնացքով:
Yes ayntegh kgnam gnats'k'ov.

202 - 2

This is a great chance.
Սա մեծ հնարավորություն է:
Sa mets hnaravorut'yun e.

202 - 3

I have made a mistake.
Ես սխալվել եմ.
Yes skhalvel yem.

202 - 4

Does he have a pulse?
Նա ունի՞ զարկերակ:
Na uni˚ zarkerak:

202 - 5

How old is he?
Քանի տարեկան է նա?
K'ani tarekan e na?

202 - 6

Turn headlights on.
Միացրեք լուսարձակները:
Miats'rek' lusardzaknery:

202 - 7

Speak louder, please.
Ավելի բարձր խոսիր, խնդրում եմ:
Aveli bardzr khosir, khndrum yem.

Day 202

Test 29

203 - 1

My shoes got dirty.

203 - 2

It is as you say.

203 - 3

I bought three glasses.

203 - 4

I don't have time now.

29/52

203 - 5

I'm starving.

203 - 6

I'll go there by train.

203 - 7

Speak louder, please.

Day 203

Week 30

204 - 1

She is not that stupid.

Նա այնքան էլ հիմար չէ:

Na aynk'an el himar ch'e:

204 - 2

It is a heart attack.

Դա սրտի կաթված է:

Da srti kat'vats e.

204 - 3

I don't care.

Ինձ չի հետաքրքրում:

Indz ch'i hetak'rk'rum:

204 - 4

He is my grandfather.

Նա իմ պապիկն է:

Na im papikn e.

204 - 5

Why did you call him?

Ինչու եք զանգահարել նրան:

Inch'u yek' zangaharel nran.

204 - 6

Don't eat too much.

Շատ մի կերեք:

Shat mi kerek':

204 - 7

I am very strict.

Ես շատ խիստ եմ:

Yes shat khist yem.

Day 204

Week 30

205 - 1

Call a fire brigade!

Զանգահարե՛ք հրշեջ բրիգադ:

Zangahare`k' hrshej brigad.

205 - 2

What is the first step?

Ո՞րն է առաջին քայլը:

VO˝rn e arrajin k`ayly:

205 - 3

What is your score?

Ո՞րն է ձեր միավորը:

VO˝rn e dzer miavory:

205 - 4

Don't move with them.

Մի շարժվեք նրանց հետ:

Mi sharzhvek' nrants' het:

30/52

205 - 5

What a letdown.

Ինչպիսի հիասթափություն:

Inch`pisi hiast`ap`ut`yun:

205 - 6

May I have a fork?

Կարո՞ղ եմ պատառաքաղ ունենալ:

Karo˝gh yem patarrak`agh unenal:

205 - 7

I'm in a lot of pain.

Ես շատ եմ ցավում:

Yes shat yem ts`avum:

Day 205

Week 30

206 - 1

Ice floats on water.

Սառույցը լողում է ջրի վրա:

Sarruyts'y loghum e jri vra.

206 - 2

I had a great time.

Ես շատ լավ ժամանակ անցկացրի:

Yes shat lav zhamanak ants'kats'ri:

206 - 3

They have guns.

Նրանք զենքեր ունեն:

Nrank' zenk'er unen.

206 - 4

Are the shops open?

Խանութները բաց են?

Khanut'nery bats' yen?

30/52

206 - 5

This is a shortcut.

Սա դյուրանցում է:

Sa dyurants'um e:

206 - 6

His car is new.

Նրա մեքենան նոր է:

Nra mek'enan nor e.

206 - 7

Where do you live?

Որտեղ ես ապրում?

Vortegh yes aprum?

Day 206

Week 30

207 - 1

Is it true?

Արդյոք դա ճիշտ է?

Ardyok' da chisht e?

207 - 2

Don't make me angry.

Ինձ մի բարկացիր:

Indz mi barkats'ir.

207 - 3

Don't rush me.

Մի շտապիր ինձ:

Mi shtapir indz:

207 - 4

The traffic is clear.

Երթեւեկությունը պարզ է.

Yert'evekut'yuny parz e.

207 - 5

I prefer reading books.

Ես նախընտրում եմ գրքեր կարդալ:

Yes nakhyntrum yem grk'er kardal.

207 - 6

I return home at 6.30.

Ես տուն եմ վերադառնում 6.30-ին:

Yes tun yem veradarrnum 6.30-in.

207 - 7

Can you forgive me?

Կարող եք ներել ինձ:

Karogh yek' nerel indz:

Day 207

Week 30

208 - 1

Don't try my patience.

Մի փորձիր իմ համբերությունը։

Mi p'vordzir im hamberut'yuny:

208 - 2

Any message please?

Խնդրում եմ, որևէ հաղորդագրություն։

Khndrum yem, voreve haghordagrut'yun:

208 - 3

The scenery is great.

Տեսարանը հիանալի է։

Tesarany hianali e.

208 - 4

Hide it up somewhere.

Թաքցնել այն ինչ-որ տեղ։

T'ak'ts'nel ayn inch'-vor tegh:

208 - 5

We are six persons.

Մենք վեց հոգի ենք։

Menk' vets' hogi yenk'.

208 - 6

I'm lending him a book.

Ես նրան գիրք եմ տալիս։

Yes nran girk' yem talis:

208 - 7

Her skin is very white.

Նրա մաշկը շատ սպիտակ է։

Nra mashky shat spitak e:

Day 208

Week 30

209 - 1

It's 6 A.M now.

Հիմա ժամը 6-ն է:

Hima zhamy 6-n e:

209 - 2

I guarantee your safety.

Ես երաշխավորում եմ ձեր անվտանգությունը:

Yes yerashkhavorum yem dzer anvtangut'yuny:

209 - 3

I missed the bus.

Ես բաց եմ թողել ավտոբուսը:

Yes bats' yem t'voghel avtobusy.

209 - 4

I totally disagree.

Ես բացարձակապես համաձայն չեմ:

Yes bats'ardzakapes hamadzayn ch'em:

30/52

209 - 5

Let's take a break.

Եկեք ընդմիջենք:

Yekek' yndmijenk':

209 - 6

You are not allowed to.

Ձեզ թույլ չեն տալիս:

DZez t'uyl ch'en talis.

209 - 7

Here is your tip.

Ահա ձեր հուշումը.

Aha dzer hushumy.

Day 209

Test 30

210 - 1

Don't eat too much.

210 - 2

What a letdown.

210 - 3

Are the shops open?

210 - 4

Don't rush me.

30/52

210 - 5

Any message please?

210 - 6

It's 6 A.M now.

210 - 7

Here is your tip.

Day 210

Week 31

211 - 1

He has long legs.

Նա երկար ոտքեր ունի:

Na yerkar votk'er uni.

211 - 2

That's awful.

Դա ահավոր է.

Da ahavor e.

211 - 3

I am outspoken.

Ես անկեղծ եմ ասում.

Yes ankeghts yem asum.

211 - 4

These grapes are sour.

Այս խաղողը թթու է:

Ays khaghoghy t't'u e.

31/52

211 - 5

He has office today.

Նա այսօր գրասենյակ ունի:

Na aysor grasenyak uni.

211 - 6

I'm scared of snakes.

Ես վախենում եմ օձերից.

Yes vakhenum yem odzerits'.

211 - 7

Take care.

Խնամել.

Khnamel.

Day 211

Week 31

212 - 1

Read it out loud.

Կարդացեք այն բարձրաձայն:

Kardats'ek' ayn bardzradzayn:

212 - 2

Our team lost the game.

Մեր թիմը պարտվեց խաղում.

Mer t'imy partvets' khaghum.

212 - 3

My friend is over there.

Իմ ընկերն այնտեղ է:

Im ynkern ayntegh e:

212 - 4

How tall are you?

Որքան է հասակդ?

Vork'an e hasakd?

212 - 5

Drink plenty of water.

Շատ ջուր խմեք:

Shat jur khmek'.

212 - 6

He stood on stage.

Նա կանգնեց բեմի վրա:

Na kangnets' bemi vra.

212 - 7

Please calm down.

Խնդրում եմ հանգստացիր:

Khndrum yem hangstats'ir.

Day 212

Week 31

213 - 1

What is your name?

Ինչ է քո անունը?

Inch' e k'vo anuny?

213 - 2

Be careful.

Զգույշ եղիր.

Zguysh yeghir.

213 - 3

What does it mean?

Ինչ է դա նշանակում?

Inch' e da nshanakum?

213 - 4

I can't breathe.

Ես չեմ կարողանում շնչել:

Yes ch'em karoghanum shnch'el.

31/52

213 - 5

I don't like him.

Ես նրան չեմ սիրում:

Yes nran ch'em sirum.

213 - 6

Are you afraid of them?

Դուք վախենում եք նրանցից:

Duk' vakhenum yek' nrants'its':

213 - 7

You can go home.

Դուք կարող եք գնալ տուն:

Duk' karogh yek' gnal tun:

Day 213

Week 31

214 - 1

Do you have any doubt?

Դուք կասկած ունե՞ք:

Duk' kaskats une"k'.

214 - 2

Is this organic?

Սա օրգանի՞կ է:

Sa organi"k e:

214 - 3

I got an email from him.

Ես նրանից նամակ ստացա:

Yes nranits' namak stats'a:

214 - 4

My father's a lawyer.

Հայրս փաստաբան է:

Hayrs p'astaban e.

214 - 5

31/52

This cup is plastic.

Այս բաժակը պլաստիկ է:

Ays bazhaky plastik e.

214 - 6

She said so.

Նա այդպես ասաց:

Na aydpes asats':

214 - 7

The road is closed.

Ճանապարհը փակ է.

Chanaparhy p'ak e.

Day 214

Week 31

215 - 1

Which is the sauce?
Ո՞րն է սոուսը:
VO°rn e sousy:

215 - 2

I am always positive.
Ես միշտ դրական եմ տրամադրված:
Yes misht drakan yem tramadrvats.

215 - 3

I am retired.
Ես թոշակառու եմ:
Yes t'voshakarru yem.

215 - 4

I've been attacked.
Ինձ վրա հարձակվել են.
Indz vra hardzakvel yen.

31/52

215 - 5

He dared to face danger.
Նա համարձակվեց դիմակայել վտանգի:
Na hamardzakvets' dimakayel vtangi.

215 - 6

Stay with me.
Մնա ինձ հետ.
Mna indz het.

215 - 7

My mother sighed.
Մայրս հառաչեց.
Mayrs harrach'ets'.

Day 215

Week 31

216 - 1

I write right-handed.

Ես գրում եմ աջ ձեռքով.

Yes grum yem aj dzerrk'ov.

216 - 2

Yes, I'd love to.

Այո, ես կցանկանայի:

Ayo, yes kts'ankanayi:

216 - 3

That was a great match!

Դա հիանալի հանդիպում էր:

Da hianali handipum er:

216 - 4

Her words hurt me.

Նրա խոսքերն ինձ ցավ պատճառեցին:

Nra khosk'ern indz ts'av patcharrets'in.

216 - 5

31/52

What have you decided?

Ի՞նչ եք որոշել:

I°nch' yek' voroshel.

216 - 6

Who is still answering?

Ո՞վ է դեռ պատասխանում.

VO°v e derr pataskhanum.

216 - 7

The baby is smiling.

Երեխան ժպտում է.

Yerekhan zhptum e.

Day 216

Test 31

217 - 1

I'm scared of snakes.

217 - 2

Drink plenty of water.

217 - 3

I can't breathe.

217 - 4

I got an email from him.

31/52

217 - 5

I am always positive.

217 - 6

I write right-handed.

217 - 7

The baby is smiling.

Day 217

Week 32

218 - 1

You're fired.

Դուք ազատված եք աշխատանքից:

Duk' azatvats yek' ashkhatank'its':

218 - 2

He came on Wednesday.

Նա եկավ չորեքշաբթի օրը:

Na yekav ch'vorek'shabt'i ory.

218 - 3

The water is hard.

Ջուրը կոշտ է:

Jury kosht e.

218 - 4

I have to go now.

Ես հիմա պետք է գնամ:

Yes hima petk' e gnam.

218 - 5

The pool is packed.

Լողավազանը լեփ-լեցուն է:

Loghavazany lep'-letc'un e.

218 - 6

It's raining.

Անձրև է գալիս:

Andzrev e galis.

218 - 7

I work from home.

Ես աշխատում եմ տնից:

Yes ashkhatum yem tnits'.

Day 218

Week 32

219 - 1

I am an Engineer.

Ես ինժեներ եմ.

Yes inzhener yem.

219 - 2

A table for two?

Սեղան երկուսի համար?

Seghan yerkusi hamar?

219 - 3

He has a rich spirit.

Նա հարուստ ոգի ունի:

Na harust vogi uni.

219 - 4

Solve it on the board.

Լուծեք այն գրատախտակի վրա:

Lutsek' ayn gratakhtaki vra:

32/52

219 - 5

It's been a long time.

Երկար ժամանակ է անցել:

Yerkar zhamanak e ants'el.

219 - 6

I had a scary dream.

Ես սարսափելի երազ տեսա.

Yes sarsap'eli yeraz tesa.

219 - 7

Don't do it again.

Այլևս մի արեք դա:

Aylevs mi arek' da:

Day 219

Week 32

220 - 1

May I use your computer?

Կարո՞դ եմ օգտագործել ձեր համակարգիչը:

Karo"gh yem ogtagortsel dzer hamakargich'y:

220 - 2

I saw his album.

Ես տեսա նրա ալբոմը:

Yes tesa nra albomy.

220 - 3

They speak French.

Նրանք խոսում են ֆրանսերեն:

Nrank' khosum yen franseren:

220 - 4

Have a drink.

Խմել.

Khmel.

220 - 5

A pinch of salt.

Մի պտղունց աղ:

Mi ptghunts' aylı.

32/52

220 - 6

I got drunk last night.

Երեկ երեկոյան ես հարբել եմ:

Yerek yerekoyan yes harbel yem.

220 - 7

My father loves fishing.

Հայրս սիրում է ձկնորսություն:

Hayrs sirum e dzknorsut'yun.

Day 220

Week 32

221 - 1

Nice of you to make it.

Հաճելի է, որ դա արեցիք:

Hacheli e, vor da arets'ik':

221 - 2

Did you pass the exam?

Դուք հանձնե՞լ եք քննությունը:

Duk' handzne"l yek' k'nnut'yuny:

221 - 3

The steak looks rare.

Սթեյքը հազվադեպ է թվում:

St'eyk'y hazvadep e t'vum:

221 - 4

I'm 27 years old.

Ես 27 տարեկան եմ:

Yes 27 tarekan yem.

221 - 5

32/52

Go straight on.

Ուղիղ գնամ.

Ughigh gnam.

221 - 6

The brown bag is mine.

Շագանակագույն պայուսակն իմն է:

Shaganakaguyn payusakn imn e.

221 - 7

No, I'd rather not.

Ոչ, ես կնախընտրեի ոչ:

Voch', yes knakhyntrev voch':

Day 221

Week 32

222 - 1

We come from Paris.

Մենք գալիս ենք Փարիզից:

Menk' galis yenk' P'arizits'.

222 - 2

It's midnight.

Կեսգիշեր է:

Kesgisher e.

222 - 3

The building collapsed.

Շենքը փլուզվել է.

SHenk'y p'luzvel e.

222 - 4

I can't avoid it.

Ես չեմ կարող խուսափել դրանից:

Yes ch'em karogh khusap'el dranits'.

222 - 5

Is this reduced?

Սա կրճատվե՞լ է:

Sa krchatvo°l e:

32/52

222 - 6

No one knows that story.

Ոչ ոք չգիտի այդ պատմությունը:

Voch' vok' ch'giti ayd patmut'yuny.

222 - 7

Did she ask me?

Նա ինձ հարցրե՞լ է:

Na indz harts're°l e:

Day 222

Week 32

223 - 1

I was shocked to hear.

Ես ցնցված էի լսելով.

Yes ts'nts'vats ei lselov.

223 - 2

You are all set.

Դուք ամեն ինչ պատրաստ եք:

Duk' amen inch' patrast yek':

223 - 3

The child woke up.

Երեխան արթնացավ.

Yerekhan art'nats'av.

223 - 4

Keep yourself cool.

Ձեզ զով պահեք:

DZez zov pahek':

32/52

223 - 5

Do you know his name?

Գիտե՞ք նրա անունը:

Gite"k' nra anuny.

223 - 6

I will call for help.

Ես օգնություն կկանչեմ.

Yes ognut'yun kkanch'em.

223 - 7

He tried an experiment.

Նա փորձարկեց.

Na p'vordzarkets'.

Day 223

Test 32

224 - 1

It's raining.

224 - 2

It's been a long time.

224 - 3

Have a drink.

224 - 4

The steak looks rare.

224 - 5

It's midnight.

32/52

224 - 6

I was shocked to hear.

224 - 7

He tried an experiment.

Day 224

Week 33

225 - 1

Does the boy arise?
Արդյո՞ք տղան առաջանում է:
Ardyo°k' tghan arrajanum e:

225 - 2

Close the door properly.
Դուռը պատշաճ կերպով փակեք:
Durry patshach kerpov p'akek'.

225 - 3

He said in a low voice.
Նա ցածրաձայն ասաց.
Na ts'atsradzayn asats'.

225 - 4

This is for you.
Սա ձեզ համար է:
Sa dzez hamar e:

33/52

225 - 5

My head is spinning.
Գլուխս պտտվում է:
Glukhs pttvum e.

225 - 6

Please check the tyres.
Խնդրում ենք ստուգել անվադողերը:
Khndrum yenk' stugel anvadoghery:

225 - 7

I have a meeting today.
Ես այսոր հանդիպում ունեմ:
Yes aysor handipum unem.

Day 225

Week 33

226 - 1

Does the dog bite?
Շունը կծու՞մ է:
Shuny ktsuⁿm e:

226 - 2

I bought a new computer.
Ես նոր համակարգիչ եմ գնել:
Yes nor hamakargich' yem gnel.

226 - 3

He has thick eyebrows.
Նա հաստ հոնքեր ունի:
Na hast honk'er uni.

226 - 4

His movements are quick.
Նրա շարժումները արագ են:
Nra sharzhumnery arag yen.

226 - 5

I peeled a carrot.
Ես գազար մաքրեցի:
Yes gazar mak'rota'i·

33/52

226 - 6

I like strong tastes.
Ես սիրում եմ ուժեղ համեր:
Yes sirum yem uzhegh hamer.

226 - 7

The test was very easy.
Թեստը շատ հեշտ էր.
T'esty shat hesht er.

Day 226

Week 33

227 - 1

May I borrow your book?

Կարո՞ղ եմ վերցնել ձեր գիրքը:

Karo"gh yem verts'nel dzer girk'y:

227 - 2

Please breathe slowly.

Խնդրում եմ դանդաղ շնչեք:

Khndrum yem dandagh shnch'ek':

227 - 3

Please stand up.

Խնդրում եմ վեր կացեք:

Khndrum yem ver kats'ek'.

227 - 4

He's a careful person.

Նա զգույշ մարդ է:

Na zguysh mard e:

227 - 5

I know how it feels.

Ես գիտեմ, թե ինչ է դա զգում:

Yes gitem, t'e inch' e da zgum:

227 - 6

I am terrified.

Ես սարսափած եմ:

Yes sarsap'ats yem.

227 - 7

What's the problem?

Ինչումն է խնդիրը?

Inch'umn e khndiry?

Day 227

Week 33

228 - 1

I handed him the letter.

Ես նրան հանձնեցի նամակը։

Yes nran handznets'i namaky.

228 - 2

Please pass me the salt.

Խնդրում եմ, փոխանցիր ինձ աղը։

Khndrum yem, p'vokhants'ir indz aghy:

228 - 3

Please give an example.

Խնդրում եմ օրինակ բերեք։

Khndrum yem orinak berek'.

228 - 4

When can I talk to you?

Ե՞րբ կարող եմ խոսել ձեզ հետ։

Ye°rb karogh yem khosel dzez het:

228 - 5

He fired the servant.

Նա աշխատանքից ազատեց ծառային։

Na aghkhhatank'its' azatots' tsarrayin.

33/52

228 - 6

He has weekdays off.

Նա հանգստյան օրեր ունի։

Na hangstyan orer uni:

228 - 7

Whatever you want.

Ամենը, ինչ կցանկանաք.

Ameny, inch' kts'ankanak'.

Day 228

Week 33

229 - 1

Right of way changed.

Ճանապարհի իրավունքը փոխվել է.

Chanaparhi iravunk'y p'vokhvel e.

229 - 2

This is a small town.

Սա փոքրիկ քաղաք է:

Sa p'vok'rik k'aghak' e.

229 - 3

Everyone has flaws.

Բոլորն էլ ունեն թերություններ:

Bolorn el unen t'erut'yunner:

229 - 4

It's good to see you.

Հաճելի է քեզ տեսնել:

Hacheli e k'ez tesnel:

33/52

229 - 5

Is this on sale?

Սա վաճառվո՞ւմ է:

Sa vacharrvo°wm e:

229 - 6

How are things?

Ինչպես են գործերը?

Inch'pes yen gortsery?

229 - 7

Good morning.

Բարի առավոտ.

Bari arravot.

Day 229

Week 33

230 - 1

I told him everything.

Ես նրան ամեն ինչ ասացի:

Yes nran amen inch' asats'i.

230 - 2

What a beautiful person!

Ի՞նչ գեղեցիկ մարդ է:

I˜nch' geghets'ik mard e.

230 - 3

He became a doctor.

Նա դարձավ բժիշկ:

Na dardzav bzhishk.

230 - 4

Do you play any sports?

Զբաղվու՞մ եք որևէ սպորտաձևով:

Zbaghvu˜m yek' voreve sportadzevov:

230 - 5

Do not smoke.

Չծխել.

Ch'tskhel.

33/52

230 - 6

You're wrong.

Դուք սխալվում եք:

Duk' skhalvum yek':

230 - 7

Sorry, it's my fault.

Կներեք, դա իմ մեղքն է:

Knerek', da im meghk'n e:

Day 230

Test 33

231 - 1

Please check the tyres.

231 - 2

I peeled a carrot.

231 - 3

He's a careful person.

231 - 4

Please give an example.

33/52

231 - 5

This is a small town.

231 - 6

I told him everything.

231 - 7

Sorry, it's my fault.

Day 231

Week 34

232 - 1

A dash of pepper.

Մի բաժակ պղպեղ:

Mi bazhak pghpegh:

232 - 2

I resemble my mother.

Ես նման եմ մորս.

Yes nman yem mors.

232 - 3

Which do you like best?

Ո՞րն է ձեզ ամենաշատը դուր գալիս:

VO˚rn e dzez amenashaty dur galis:

232 - 4

I like watching T.V.

Ես սիրում եմ դիտել T.V.

Yes sirum yem ditel T.V.

232 - 5

Let's meet again.

Եկեք նորից հանդիպենք:

Yekek' norits' handipenk'.

34/52

232 - 6

Do you have a pen?

Դուք գրիչ ունե՞ք:

Duk' grich' une˚k':

232 - 7

Why are you laughing?

Ինչու ես ծիծաղում?

Inch'u yes tsitsaghum?

Day 232

Week 34

233 - 1

He works at an embassy.

Նա աշխատում է դեսպանատանը:

Na ashkhatum e despanatany.

233 - 2

He's a nasty man.

Նա զզվելի մարդ է:

Na zzveli mard e:

233 - 3

We can't do it here.

Մենք չենք կարող դա անել այստեղ:

Menk' ch'enk' karogh da anel aystegh:

233 - 4

Did he award him?

Արդյո°ք նա նրան պարգեվատրել է:

Ardyo°k' na nran pargevatrel e:

233 - 5

34/52

He was very helpful.

Նա շատ օգտակար էր:

Na shat ogtakar er:

233 - 6

Can we meet next Friday?

Կարո°ղ ենք հանդիպել հաջորդ ուրբաթ:

Karo°gh yenk' handipel hajord urbat':

233 - 7

I got a new job.

Ես նոր աշխատանք գտա.

Yes nor ashkhatank' gta.

Day 233

Week 34

234 - 1

Kiss me, my darling.

Համբուրիր ինձ, սիրելիս:

Hamburir indz, sirelis:

234 - 2

Everybody is fine.

Բոլորը լավ են:

Bolory lav yen.

234 - 3

What's your surname?

Ի՞նչ է Ձեր ազգանունը?

Inch' e DZer azganuny?

234 - 4

Please help yourself.

Խնդրում եմ օգնեք ինքներդ ձեզ:

Khndrum yem ognek' ink'nerd dzez:

234 - 5

Milk was sold out.

Կաթը սպառվել է.

Kat'y sparrvel e.

34/52

234 - 6

He's a serious student.

Նա լուրջ ուսանող է:

Na lurj usanogh e:

234 - 7

Your guest has arrived.

Ձեր հյուրը եկել է:

DZer hyury yekel e:

Day 234

Week 34

235 - 1

I belong to Chicago.

Ես պատկանում եմ Չիկագոյին:

Yes patkanum yem Ch'ikagoyin.

235 - 2

Please come here.

Խնդրում եմ արի այստեղ:

Khndrum yem ari aystegh.

235 - 3

He owes me one.

Նա ինձ մեկ պարտական է:

Na indz mek partakan e:

235 - 4

Is he running?

Նա վազո՞ւմ է:

Na vazo°wm e.

235 - 5

You look very handsome.

Դուք շատ գեղեցիկ տեսք ունեք:

Duk' shat geghets'ik tesk' unek'.

235 - 6

I am a housewife.

Ես տնային տնտեսուհի եմ:

Yes tnayin tntesuhi yem.

235 - 7

Are you ready to order?

Պատրա՞ստ եք պատվիրել:

Patra°st yek' patvirel.

Day 235

Week 34

236 - 1

I'm impressed.

Ես տպավորված եմ։

Yes tpavorvats yem.

236 - 2

Call an ambulance.

Շտապ օգնություն կանչեք։

Shtap ognut'yun kanch'ek'.

236 - 3

Where's the post office?

Որտե՞ղ է փոստային բաժանմունքը։

Vorte°gh e p'vostayin bazhanmunk'y:

236 - 4

Where are you working?

Որտե՞ղ ես աշխատում։

Vorte°gh yes ashkhatum.

236 - 5

He's good at baseball.

Նա լավ է բեյսբոլում։

Na lav e beysbolum:

34/52

236 - 6

How is your father?

Ինչպե՞ս է ձեր հայրը։

Inch'pe°s e dzer hayry:

236 - 7

Don't be afraid.

Մի՛ վախեցիր։

Mi՛ vakhets'ir.

Day 236

Week 34

237 - 1

She shed tears.

Նա արցունքներ թափեց։

Na arts'unk'ner t'ap'ets'.

237 - 2

Can you hear me?

Լսո՞ւմ ես ինձ։

Lso"wm yes indz.

237 - 3

This road is bumpy.

Այս ճանապարհը խորդուբորդ է.

Ays chanaparhy khordubord e.

237 - 4

What time can we meet?

Ո՞ր ժամին կարող ենք հանդիպել։

VO"r zhamin karogh yenk' handipel:

237 - 5

Lock the door.

Կողպեք դուռը։

Koghpek' durry:

34/52

237 - 6

The room light is on.

Սենյակի լույսը վառված է։

Senyaki luysy varrvats e.

237 - 7

See you tomorrow.

Կտեսնվենք վաղը.

Ktesnvenk' vaghy.

Day 237

Test 34

238 - 1

Do you have a pen?

238 - 2

He was very helpful.

238 - 3

Please help yourself.

238 - 4

He owes me one.

238 - 5

Call an ambulance.

238 - 6

She shed tears.

238 - 7

See you tomorrow.

Day 238

Week 35

239 - 1

No stopping.

Ո՛չ մի կանգառ:

Voch' mi kangarr:

239 - 2

The meeting is closed.

Հանդիպումը փակ է.

Handipumy p'ak e.

239 - 3

How are you doing?

Ինչպես ես?

Inch'pes yes?

239 - 4

Whom do you suspect?

Ո՞ւմ եք կասկածում:

VO"wm yek' kaskatsum:

239 - 5

35/52

He loaded the pistol.

Նա լիցքավորել է ատրճանակը:

Na lits'k'avorel e atrchanaky.

239 - 6

I'm absolutely sure.

Ես միանգամայն վստահ եմ.

Yes miangamayn vstah yem.

239 - 7

I started a new job.

Ես սկսեցի նոր աշխատանք.

Yes sksets'i nor ashkhatank'.

Day 239

Week 35

240 - 1

What can you say?

Ի՞նչ կարող ես ասել։

I'nch' karogh yes asel.

240 - 2

Open wide, please.

Լայն բացեք, խնդրում եմ։

Layn bats'ek', khndrum yem.

240 - 3

What time do you open?

Ո՞ր ժամին եք բացում։

VO'r zhamin yek' bats'um:

240 - 4

I go to bed at 10.30.

Ես գնում եմ քնելու 10.30-ին։

Yes gnum yem k'nelu 10.30-in.

240 - 5

It is straight ahead.

Դա ուղիղ առջև է։

Da ughigh arrjev e:

35/52

240 - 6

Wonderful, thank you.

Հրաշալի է, շնորհակալություն։

Hrashali e, shnorhakalut'yun.

240 - 7

I didn't do it.

Ես դա չեմ արել։

Yes da ch'em arel.

Day 240

Week 35

241 - 1

A person is missing.
Մարդը բացակայում է.
Mardy bats'akayum e.

241 - 2

He is in debt.
Նա պարտքերի մեջ է:
Na partk'eri mej e.

241 - 3

Good afternoon.
Բարի օր.
Bari or.

241 - 4

I have two brothers.
Ես երկու եղբայր ունեմ.
Yes yerku yeghbayr unem.

241 - 5

He has six children.
Նա ունի վեց երեխա:
Na uni vets' yerekha.

35/52

241 - 6

Do not lean.
Մի թեքվեք.
Mi t'ek'vek'.

241 - 7

Her hair is very long.
Նրա մազերը շատ երկար են:
Nra mazery shat yerkar yen.

Day 241

Week 35

242 - 1

He is my elder brother.

Նա իմ ավագ եղբայրն է:

Na im avag yeghbayrn e.

242 - 2

The sweater has shrunk.

Սվիտերը կօկվել է:

Svitery ktskvel e.

242 - 3

I don't agree with you.

Ես համաձայն չեմ քեզ հետ:

Yes hamadzayn ch'em k'ez het.

242 - 4

I don't have some cash.

Ես կանխիկ գումար չունեմ:

Yes kankhik gumar ch'unem:

242 - 5

She's a quick learner.

Նա արագ սովորող է:

Na arag sovorogh e:

35/52

242 - 6

My son is now a toddler.

Իմ տղան այժմ փոքր երեխա է:

Im tghan ayzhm p'vok'r yerekha e:

242 - 7

I work as a Professor.

Ես աշխատում եմ որպես պրոֆեսոր:

Yes ashkhatum yem vorpes profesor.

Day 242

Week 35

243 - 1

I owe you a great deal.

Ես քեզ շատ եմ պարտական:

Yes k'ez shat yem partakan:

243 - 2

Oh, my god. Really?

O, աստված իմ: Իսկապե՞ս:

O, astvats im: Iskape˚s:

243 - 3

Hazardous waste.

Վտանգավոր թափոններ.

Vtangavor t'ap'vonner.

243 - 4

That child is so thin.

Այդ երեխան այնքան նիհար է:

Ayd yerekhan aynk'an nihar e:

243 - 5

Let's bring some water.

Եկեք մի քիչ ջուր բերենք:

Yekek' mi k'ich' jur berenk'.

243 - 6

Don't confuse me.

Ինձ մի շփոթեք.

Indz mi shp'vot'ek'.

243 - 7

Follow the signs.

Հետևեք նշաններին.

Hetevek' nshannerin.

Day 243

35/52

Week 35

244 - 1

She despised him.

Նա արհամարհում էր նրան:

Na arhamarhum er nran.

244 - 2

Let it go.

Թող գնա.

T'vogh gna.

244 - 3

Don't play on the road.

Մի խաղացեք ճանապարհի վրա:

Mi khaghats'ek' chanaparhi vra:

244 - 4

I work in healthcare.

Ես աշխատում եմ առողջապահության ոլորտում:

Yes ashkhatum yem arroghjapahut'yan volortum.

244 - 5

I got a perfect score.

Ես ստացա կատարյալ միավոր:

Yes stats'a kataryal miavor.

35/52

244 - 6

I'm looking for my dog.

Ես փնտրում եմ իմ շանը:

Yes p'ntrum yem im shany.

244 - 7

What's happening?

Ինչ է կատարվում?

Inch' e katarvum?

Day 244

Test 35

245 - 1

I'm absolutely sure.

245 - 2

It is straight ahead.

245 - 3

I have two brothers.

245 - 4

I don't agree with you.

245 - 5

Oh, my god. Really?

35/52

245 - 6

She despised him.

245 - 7

What's happening?

Day 245

Week 36

246 - 1

The steak here is OK.

Սթեյքն այստեղ լավ է:

St'eyk'n aystegh lav e:

246 - 2

I want to gain weight.

Ես ուզում եմ գիրանալ.

Yes uzum yem giranal.

246 - 3

A new year has started.

Նոր տարի է սկսվել.

Nor tari e sksvel.

246 - 4

Have you heard the news?

Լսե՞լ եք լուրը:

Lse°l yek' lury.

246 - 5

She is nearsighted.

Նա կարՃատես է:

Na karohntes e.

36/52

246 - 6

He should exercise more.

Նա պետք է ավելի շատ մարզվի:

Na petk' e aveli shat marzvi:

246 - 7

Good to see you.

Ուրախ եմ քեզ տեսնել.

Urakh yem k'ez tesnel.

Day 246

Week 36

247 - 1

Are you on time?
Դուք ժամանակին եք:
Duk' zhamanakin yek':

247 - 2

She was very pleased.
Նա շատ գոհ էր:
Na shat goh er:

247 - 3

My son turned six.
Տղաս դարձավ վեց տարեկան:
Tghas dardzav vets' tarekan.

247 - 4

Where do they live?
Որտեղ են նրանք ապրում?
Vortegh yen nrank' aprum?

36/52

247 - 5

I get up at 6.30.
Ես վեր եմ կենում 6.30-ին:
Yes ver yem kenum 6.30-in.

247 - 6

Before you think, try.
Նախքան մտածելը, փորձիր:
Nakhk'an mtatsely, p'vordzir.

247 - 7

May I offer you a drink?
Կարո՞ղ եմ ձեզ խմել:
Karo°gh yem dzez khmel:

Day 247

Week 36

248 - 1

Have dinner.

Ճաշել.

Chashel.

248 - 2

Do not stare at people.

Մի՛ նայիր մարդկանց.

Mi՛ nayir mardkants'.

248 - 3

That's too expensive.

Դա չափազանց թանկ է:

Da ch'ap'azants' t'ank e:

248 - 4

Can you show me how to?

Կարո՞ղ եք ինձ ցույց տալ, թե ինչպես:

Karo՞gh yek' indz ts'uyts' tal, t'e inch'pes:

248 - 5

Put on your boots!

Հագի՛ր կոշիկներդ:

Hagi՛r koshiknerd.

36/52

248 - 6

It is nothing.

Դա ոչինչ է:

Da voch'inch' e.

248 - 7

That was excellent.

Դա գերազանց էր:

Da gerazants' er:

Day 248

Week 36

249 - 1

Sure. I'll come.

Իհարկե: Ես կգամ:

Iharke: yes kgam.

249 - 2

He is on the other line.

Նա մյուս գծում է:

Na myus gtsum e.

249 - 3

I'm finished.

Ես վերջացրի.

Yes verjats'ri.

249 - 4

I'll go.

Ես կգնամ:

Yes kgnam.

249 - 5

The flu spread rapidly.

Գրիպը արագ տարածվեց:

Gripy arag taratsvets'.

36/52

249 - 6

Don't talk to me.

Ինձ հետ մի խոսիր:

Indz het mi khosir.

249 - 7

First day of school.

Դպրոցական առաջին օրը.

Dprots'akan arrajin ory.

Day 249

Week 36

250 - 1

He's a rational person.

Նա ռացիոնալ մարդ է:

Na rrats'ional mard e:

250 - 2

He has no time.

Նա ժամանակ չունի:

Na zhamanak ch'uni.

250 - 3

Let's go by bus.

Գնանք ավտոբուսով:

Gnank' avtobusov.

250 - 4

What a cheeky fellow!

Ինչպիսի լկտի մարդ:

Inch'pisi lkti mard.

250 - 5

Can I leave my bag here?

Կարո՞ղ եմ պայուսակս այստեղ թողնել:

Karo'gh yem payusaks aysteghi t'voghnel.

36/52

250 - 6

It is really disgusting.

Իսկապես զզվելի է:

Iskapes zzveli e.

250 - 7

That's too bad.

Դա շատ վատ է.

Da shat vat e.

Day 250

Week 36

251 - 1

How tall is that tower?

Որքա՞ն է այդ աշտարակի բարձրությունը:

Vork'a"n e ayd ashtaraki bardzrut'yuny:

251 - 2

I'm from Roma.

Ես Ռոմայից եմ:

Yes Rromayits' yem:

251 - 3

Is this book good?

Այս գիրքը լավն է:

Ays girk'y lavn e:

251 - 4

My mother's a nurse.

Մայրս բուժքույր է:

Mayrs buzhk'uyr e:

251 - 5

The snow has piled up.

Ձյունը կուտակվել է:

Dzyuny kutakvel e.

36/52

251 - 6

Can I travel?

Կարո՞ղ եմ ճանապարհորդել:

Karo"gh yem chanaparhordel:

251 - 7

I am doing business.

Ես բիզնեսով եմ զբաղվում:

Yes biznesov yem zbaghvum.

Day 251

Test 36

252 - 1

He should exercise more.

252 - 2

I get up at 6.30.

252 - 3

Can you show me how to?

252 - 4

I'm finished.

252 - 5

He has no time.

36/52

252 - 6

How tall is that tower?

252 - 7

I am doing business.

Day 252

Week 37

253 - 1

She has a car.

Նա մեքենա ունի:

Na mek'ena uni.

253 - 2

She is my wife.

Նա իմ կինն է:

Na im kinn e.

253 - 3

It is forbidden to.

Արգելվում է.

Argelvum e.

253 - 4

No classes tomorrow.

Վաղը դասեր չկան:

Vaghy daser ch'kan:

253 - 5

Where are the shops?

Որտեղ են խանութները:

Vortegh yen khanut'nery:

253 - 6

What's new?

Ի՞նչ նորություն կա?

Inch' norut'yun ka?

253 - 7

He's very intelligent.

Նա շատ խելացի է:

Na shat khelats'i e:

Day 253

Week 37

254 - 1

What sport do you do?

Ի՞նչ սպորտով ես զբաղվում:

I˝nch' sportov yes zbaghvum.

254 - 2

I will ask them to wait.

Ես կխնդրեմ, որ սպասեն:

Yes kkhndrem, vor spasen.

254 - 3

My father yawned.

Հայրս հորանջեց.

Hayrs horanjets'.

254 - 4

Yes, I've got one.

Այո, ես ունեմ մեկը:

Ayo, yes unem meky:

254 - 5

Can I see the menu?

Կարո՞ղ եմ տեսնել ճաշացանկը:

Karo˝gh yem tesnel chrnhats'auky.

254 - 6

I have a black bag.

Ես ունեմ սև պայուսակ:

Yes unem sev payusak:

254 - 7

I have college today.

Ես այսոր քոլեջ ունեմ:

Yes aysor k'volej unem:

Day 254

Week 37

255 - 1

He combed his hair.

Նա սանրեց իր մազերը։

Na sanrets' ir mazery.

255 - 2

Will you meet me?

Կհանդիպե՞ս ինձ։

Khandipe's indz.

255 - 3

Fit as a fiddle.

Տեղավորվել որպես ջութակ։

Teghavorvel vorpes jut'ak:

255 - 4

Have a nice day!

Հաճելի օր!

Hacheli or!

255 - 5

He is very hadworking.

Նա շատ աշխատասեր է։

Na shat ashkhataser e.

37/52

255 - 6

I have mouth sores.

Ես բերանի խոցեր ունեմ։

Yes berani khots'er unem.

255 - 7

No cheating, please.

Ոչ մի խաբեություն, խնդրում եմ։

Voch' mi khabeut'yun, khndrum yem:

Day 255

Week 37

256 - 1

Call the police.

Ձանգահարեք ոստիկանություն:

Zangaharek' vostikanut'yun.

256 - 2

I'm sorry, I can't.

Կներես, չեմ կարող:

Kneres, ch'em karogh.

256 - 3

There's one problem.

Մեկ խնդիր կա.

Mek khndir ka.

256 - 4

This is my boss.

Սա իմ շեֆն է:

Sa im shefn e.

256 - 5

How is your brother?

Ինչպե՞ս է եղբայրդ:

Inch'pʿes e yeghbayrd.

256 - 6

No entry for buses.

Ավտոբուսների մուտքն արգելված է.

Avtobusneri mutk'n argelvats e.

256 - 7

Jokes do have limits.

Կատակները սահմաններ ունեն.

Kataknery sahmanner unen.

Day 256

Week 37

257 - 1

How is life?

Ինչպե՞ս է կյանքը?

Inch'pes e kyank'y?

257 - 2

Bye. Take care.

Ցտեսություն։ Խնամել.

Ts'tesut'yun. Khnamel.

257 - 3

We entered the woods.

Մենք մտանք անտառ:

Menk' mtank' antarr.

257 - 4

Who's next?

Ով է հաջորդը?

Ov e hajordy?

257 - 5

Which bus shall I take?

Ո՞ր ավտոբուսով գնամ:

VO°r avtobusov gnam:

37/52

257 - 6

How's your day?

Ինչպե՞ս է քո օրը?

Inch'pes e k'vo ory?

257 - 7

Have a safe trip back.

Անվտանգ ճանապարհորդություն վերադարձ:

Anvtang chanaparhordut'yun veradardz:

Day 257

Week 37

258 - 1

I really enjoyed it.

Ինձ շատ դուր եկավ:

Indz shat dur yekav:

258 - 2

Do not disturb.

Չխանգարել.

Ch'khangarel.

258 - 3

No homework for today.

Այսօրվա համար տնային աշխատանք չկա:

Aysorva hamar tnayin ashkhatank' ch'ka:

258 - 4

She's a busy person.

Նա զբաղված մարդ է:

Na zbaghvats mard e:

258 - 5

That girl is trendy.

Այդ աղջիկը թրենդային է:

Ayd aghjiky t'rendayin e:

258 - 6

His face was all red.

Նրա դեմքը ամբողջովին կարմիր էր:

Nra demk'y amboghjovin karmir er.

258 - 7

Here is my passport.

Ահա իմ անձնագիրը:

Aha im andznagiry.

Day 258

Test 37

259 - 1

What's new?

259 - 2

Can I see the menu?

259 - 3

Have a nice day!

259 - 4

There's one problem.

259 - 5

Bye. Take care.

37/52

259 - 6

I really enjoyed it.

259 - 7

Here is my passport.

Day 259

Week 38

260 - 1

They live a quiet life.

Նրանք ապրում են հանգիստ կյանքով:

Nrank' aprum yen hangist kyank'ov.

260 - 2

We met on the Internet.

Մենք ծանոթացանք համացանցում:

Menk' tsanot'ats'ank' hamats'ants'um.

260 - 3

I am sorry.

Կներես.

Kneres.

260 - 4

Let me check for you.

Թույլ տվեք ստուգել ձեզ համար:

T'uyl tvek' stugel dzez hamar:

260 - 5

Don't cry.

Մի լացիր:

Mi lats'ir.

38/52

260 - 6

How big is that house?

Որքա՞ն է այդ տունը:

Vork'aⁿn e ayd tuny:

260 - 7

What is his name?

Ի՞նչ է նրա անունը?

Inch' e nra anuny?

Day 260

Week 38

261 - 1

Just take it easy.

Պարզապես հանգստացեք։

Parzapes hangstats'ek':

261 - 2

My specialty is law.

Իմ մասնագիտությունը իրավաբանությունն է:

Im masnagitut'yuny iravabanut'yunn e.

261 - 3

You may now go.

Այժմ կարող եք գնալ:

Ayzhm karogh yek' gnal:

261 - 4

I get up at 5.15.

Ես վեր եմ կենում 5.15-ին:

Yes ver yem kenum 5.15-in.

261 - 5

Are you alright?

Քեզ հետ ամեն ինչ կարգին է?

K'ez het amen inch' kargin e?

38/52

261 - 6

Let's share duties.

Եկեք կիսենք պարտականությունները.

Yekek' kisenk' partakanut'yunnery.

261 - 7

No blowing of horns.

Ոչ մի շչակ.

Voch' mi shch'ak.

Day 261

Week 38

262 - 1

Good luck to you.

Հաջողություն քեզ.

Hajoghut'yun k'ez.

262 - 2

We took a package tour.

Մենք փաթեթային շրջայց կատարեցինք:

Menk' p'at'et'ayin shrjayts' katarets'ink':

262 - 3

Trust me, I can do it.

Հավատացեք ինձ, ես կարող եմ դա անել:

Havatats'ek' indz, yes karogh yem da anel:

262 - 4

It's too loose for me.

Ինձ համար դա չափազանց ազատ է:

Indz hamar da ch'ap'azants' azat e:

262 - 5

That's so sad.

Դա այնքան տխուր է:

Da aynk'an tkhur e.

38/52

262 - 6

Bear in mind.

Նկատի ունեցեք.

Nkati unets'ek'.

262 - 7

What do you suggest?

Ինչ եք առաջարկում?

Inch' yek' arrajarkum?

Day 262

Week 38

263 - 1

Goodbye.

Ցտեսություն.

Ts'tesut'yun.

263 - 2

I banged on the door.

Ես զարկեցի դուռը:

Yes zarkets'i durry.

263 - 3

I jog every day.

Ես ամեն օր վազում եմ:

Yes amen or vazum yem:

263 - 4

What day is today?

Շաբաթվա ինչ օր է այսօր?

Shabat'va inch' or e aysor?

263 - 5

See you next time.

Կտեսնվենք հաջորդ անգամ.

Ktesnvenk' hajord angam.

38/52

263 - 6

His grades went up.

Նրա գնահատականները բարձրացան:

Nra gnahatakannery bardzrats'an.

263 - 7

Are you joking?

Դու կատակում ես?

Du katakum yes?

Day 263

Week 38

264 - 1

Thank you so much!

Շատ շնորհակալություն!

Shat shnorhakalut'yun!

264 - 2

What's that?

Ինչ է դա?

Inch' e da?

264 - 3

Before you begin.

Մինչ դուք սկսեք.

Minch' duk' sksek'.

264 - 4

I feel nauseous.

Ես սրտխառնոց եմ զգում:

Yes srtkharrnots' yem zgum.

264 - 5

Can I pay by cheque?

Կարո՞ղ եմ վճարել չեկով:

Karo'gh yem vcharel ch'ekov.

264 - 6

Why is he dull?

Ինչու է նա ձանձրալի:

Inch'u e na dzandzrali:

264 - 7

This ball bounces well.

Այս գնդակը լավ է ցատկում:

Ays gndaky lav e ts'atkum:

Day 264

Week 38

265 - 1

She's studying drama.
Նա սովորում է դրամա:
Na sovorum e drama:

265 - 2

Don't be too greedy.
Շատ ագահ մի եղեք:
Shat agah mi yeghek':

265 - 3

Do you avoid me?
Դուք խուսափո՞ւմ եք ինձանից:
Duk' khusap'vo°wm yek' indzanits'.

265 - 4

Are you not well?
Լավ չես?
Lav ch'es?

265 - 5

Start the engine.
Սկսեք շարժիչը:
Sksek' sharzhich'y:

38/52

265 - 6

I have a scooter.
Ես ունեմ սկուտեր:
Yes unem skuter:

265 - 7

Who will help you?
Ո՞վ կօգնի քեզ:
VO°v kogni k'ez.

Day 265

Test 38

266 - 1

How big is that house?

266 - 2

Are you alright?

266 - 3

It's too loose for me.

266 - 4

I jog every day.

266 - 5

What's that?

266 - 6

She's studying drama.

266 - 7

Who will help you?

Day 266

Week 39

267 - 1

Put on these pajamas.

Հագեք այս գիշերազգեստները:

Hagek' ays gisherazgestnery:

267 - 2

The house is beautiful.

Տունը գեղեցիկ է:

Tuny geghets'ik e.

267 - 3

When did you call him?

Ե՞րբ եք զանգահարել նրան:

Ye°rb yek' zangaharel nran:

267 - 4

It's sorching hoait.

Դա հուգիչ է:

Da huzich' e:

267 - 5

She helped a sick dog.

Նա օգնեց հիվանդ շանը.

Na ognets' hivand shany.

267 - 6

Turn right.

Թեքվեք աջ:

T'ek'vek' aj.

267 - 7

It's my fault.

Դա իմ մեղքն է.

Da im meghk'n e.

Day 267

Week 39

268 - 1

Is he giving the book?

Նա տալիս է գիրքը:

Na talis e girk'y:

268 - 2

Is the rumor true?

Ճի՞շտ է լուրերը:

Chi°sht e lurery:

268 - 3

Are you with me?

Դու ինձ հետ ես?

Du indz het yes?

268 - 4

A kilo of fish.

Մեկ կիլոգրամ ձուկ.

Mek kilogram dzuk.

268 - 5

Don't go near him!

Նրան մի՛ մոտեցիր:

Nran mi´ mototə´ir.

268 - 6

How deep is the pool?

Որքա՞ն խորն է լողավազանը:

Vork'a°n khorn e loghavazany:

268 - 7

He studies medicine.

Բժշկություն է սովորում:

Bzhshkut'yun e sovorum.

Week 39

269 - 1

I'm quite sure about it.

Ես միանգամայն վստահ եմ դրանում:

Yes miangamayn vstah yem dranum:

269 - 2

There's a book here.

Այստեղ գիրք կա:

Aystegh girk' ka:

269 - 3

He's very popular.

Նա շատ սիրված է:

Na shat sirvats e:

269 - 4

Make a note of it.

Նշեք այն:

Nshek' ayn:

269 - 5

Open for residents.

Բաց բնակիչների համար.

Bats' bnakich'neri hamar.

269 - 6

Are you ready for this?

Պատրա՞ստ եք սրան:

Patra"st yek' sran.

269 - 7

Send him out.

Դուրս ուղարկիր նրան:

Durs ugharkir nran:

Day 269

Week 39

270 - 1

She is a bad woman.

Նա վատ կին է:

Na vat kin e.

270 - 2

It's your decision.

Դա քո որոշումն է:

Da k'vo voroshumn e:

270 - 3

Do you think it is true?

Ի՞նչ եք կարծում, դա ճի՞շտ է:

I°nch' yek' kartsum, da chi°sht e.

270 - 4

Let's talk calmly.

Եկեք հանգիստ խոսենք.

Yekek' hangist khosenk'.

270 - 5

I'm very sorry.

Շատ եմ ցավում:

Shat ynm ts'avum.

270 - 6

39/52

Help! Shark attack!

Օգնություն! Շնաձկների հարձակումը!

Ognut'yun! Shnadzkneri hardzakumy!

270 - 7

I feel lazy to get up.

Ես ծույլ եմ զգում վեր կենալու համար:

Yes tsuyl yem zgum ver kenalu hamar:

Day 270

Week 39

271 - 1

Motivate yourself.

Մոտիվացրե՛ք ինքներդ ձեզ:

Motivats're'k' ink'nerd dzez.

271 - 2

I won't go if it rains.

Ես չեմ գնա, եթե անձրն գա:

Yes ch'em gna, yet'e andzrev ga:

271 - 3

I'm truly sorry.

Ես իսկապես ցավում եմ:

Yes iskapes ts'avum yem:

271 - 4

You never listen to me.

Դու երբեք ինձ չես լսում:

Du yerbek' indz ch'es lsum:

271 - 5

What about a cup of tea?

Իսկ ի՞նչ կասեք մի բաժակ թեյի մասին:

Isk i°nch' kasek' mi bazhak t'eyi masin.

271 - 6

I need life insurance.

Ինձ կյանքի ապահովագրություն է պետք:

Indz kyank'i apahovagrut'yun e petk'.

271 - 7

Is there a bank here?

Այստեղ բանկ կա՞:

Aystegh bank ka°:

Day 271

Week 39

272 - 1

What happened?

Ի՞նչ է պատահել?

Inch' e patahel?

272 - 2

I can't move.

Ես չեմ կարող շարժվել:

Yes ch'em karogh sharzhvel:

272 - 3

I can't read a map.

Ես չեմ կարողանում քարտեզ կարդալ:

Yes ch'em karoghanum k'artez kardal.

272 - 4

Can I help you?

Կարո՞ղ եմ օգնել Ձեզ?

Karogh yem ognel DZez?

272 - 5

That's very kind of you.

Դա ձեր կողմից շատ բարի է:

Da dzer koghmits' shat bari e:

272 - 6

It's pouring down.

Այն թափվում է:

Ayn t'ap'vum e:

272 - 7

Do you have a fever?

Դուք ջերմություն ունե՞ք:

Duk' jermut'yun une°k':

Day 272

Test 39

273 - 1

Turn right.

273 - 2

Don't go near him!

273 - 3

Make a note of it.

273 - 4

Do you think it is true?

273 - 5

I won't go if it rains.

39/52

273 - 6

What happened?

273 - 7

Do you have a fever?

Day 273

Week 40

274 - 1

Who called you?

Ո՞վ է քեզ զանգահարել:

VO՞v e k'ez zangaharel:

274 - 2

Who's calling, please?

Ո՞վ է զանգում, խնդրում եմ:

VO՞v e zangum, khndrum yem:

274 - 3

I excel in this field.

Ես գերազանց եմ այս ոլորտում:

Yes gerazants' yem ays volortum:

274 - 4

I am sorry I'm late.

Կներես, որ ուշացել եմ:

Kneres, vor ushats'el yom.

274 - 5

It's very hot today.

Այսօր շատ շոգ է:

Aysor shat shog e

274 - 6

You must not.

Դուք չպետք է.

Duk' ch'petk' e.

40/52

274 - 7

How is he doing?

Ինչպե՞ս է նա:

Inch'pe՞s e na.

Day 274

Week 40

275 - 1

I didn't know that song.

Ես չգիտեի այդ երգը:

Yes ch'gitev ayd yergy.

275 - 2

I will never forget you.

Ես երբեք չեմ մոռանա քեզ.

Yes yerbek' ch'em morrana k'ez.

275 - 3

This chair is shaky.

Այս աթոռը դողում է:

Ays at'vorry doghum e:

275 - 4

I'm unemployed.

Ես գործազուրկ եմ.

Yes gortsazurk yem.

275 - 5

Nice to meet you.

Ուրախ եմ ծանոթանալու համար.

Urakh yem tsanot'analu hamar.

275 - 6

I will buy it.

Ես կգնեմ այն:

Yes kgnem ayn.

275 - 7

Don't come near me.

Մի մոտեցիր ինձ:

Mi motets'ir indz:

Day 275

Week 40

276 - 1

I don't like to wait.

Ես չեմ սիրում սպասել։

Yes ch'em sirum spasel.

276 - 2

Here you go.

Ահա դուք գնացեք։

Aha duk' gnats'ek'.

276 - 3

No entry for bicycles.

Հեծանիվների մուտքն արգելված է.

Hetsanivneri mutk'n argelvats e.

276 - 4

She is my elder sister.

Նա իմ ավագ քույրն է։

Na im avag k'uyrn e.

276 - 5

It's was nothing.

Դա ոչինչ էր։

Da voch'inch' er.

276 - 6

When is she coming?

Ե՞րբ է նա գալիս։

Ye°rb e na galis.

40/52

276 - 7

What do you think?

Ինչ՞ ես մտածում?

Inch' yes mtatsum?

Day 276

Week 40

277 - 1

Please don't be so sad.

Խնդրում եմ այդքան մի տխրիր:

Khndrum yem aydk'an mi tkhrir.

277 - 2

Monitor your weight.

Դիտեք ձեր քաշը:

Ditek' dzer k'ashy:

277 - 3

It was a touching film.

Հուզիչ ֆիլմ էր:

Huzich' film er.

277 - 4

I am a nurse.

Ես բուժքույր եմ:

Yes buzhk'uyr yem.

277 - 5

What did he say?

Ինչ է նա ասում?

Inch' e na asum?

277 - 6

40/52

He's a nice guy.

Նա լավ տղա է:

Na lav tgha e:

277 - 7

I am out for lunch.

Ես դուրս եմ եկել ճաշի:

Yes durs yem yekel chashi:

Day 277

Week 40

278 - 1

He's a very fun person.

Նա շատ զվարճալի մարդ է:

Na shat zvarchali mard e:

278 - 2

Everyone makes mistakes.

Բոլորն էլ սխալվում են:

Bolorn el skhalvum yen.

278 - 3

The house is roomy.

Տունը ընդարձակ է:

Tuny yndardzak e.

278 - 4

Eat a balanced diet.

Կերեք հավասարակշռված դիետա:

Kerek' havasarakshrrvats diyeta:

278 - 5

My soup is cold.

Իմ ապուրը սառը է:

Im apury sarry e:

278 - 6

I heard a gunshot.

Ես կրակոց լսեցի.

Yes krakots' lsets'i.

40/52

278 - 7

I agree.

Ես համաձայն եմ:

Yes hamadzayn yem.

Day 278

Week 40

279 - 1

This is absurd!

Սա աբսուրդ է:

Sa absurd e.

279 - 2

Who do you live with?

Ո՞ւմ հետ ես ապրում?

Um het yes aprum?

279 - 3

This meat is greasy.

Այս միսը յուղոտ է:

Ays misy yughot e.

279 - 4

It's pouring.

Այն հորդում է:

Ayn hordum e:

279 - 5

I have a car.

Ես մեքենա ունեմ.

Yes mek'ena unem.

279 - 6

40/52

He is doing fine.

Նա լավ է անում:

Na lav e anum:

279 - 7

Where's the station?

Որտե՞ղ է կայարանը:

Vorte°gh e kayarany:

Day 279

Test 40

280 - 1

You must not.

280 - 2

Nice to meet you.

280 - 3

She is my elder sister.

280 - 4

It was a touching film.

280 - 5

Everyone makes mistakes.

280 - 6

This is absurd!

40/52

280 - 7

Where's the station?

Day 280

Week 41

281 - 1

The bathroom is there.
Սանհանգույցը կա:

Sanhanguyts'y ka.

281 - 2

Any questions?
Հարցեր կա՞ն:

Harts'er ka῀n:

281 - 3

It's a good deal.
Դա լավ գործարք է:

Da lav gortsark' e:

281 - 4

It's too short for me.
Դա շատ կարճ է ինձ համար:

Da shat karch e indz hamar:

281 - 5

He was nervous.
Նա նյարդայնացած էր:

Na nyardaynats'ats er.

281 - 6

41/52

Where is the hospital?
Որտեղ է հիվանդանոցը:

Vortegh e hivandanots'y:

281 - 7

He runs fast.
Նա արագ է վազում:

Na arag e vazum:

Day 281

Week 41

282 - 1

I think you're wrong.

Կարծում եմ՝ սխալվում ես:

Kartsum yem՝ skhalvum yes.

282 - 2

I ate a lot of salad.

Ես շատ աղցան եմ կերել:

Yes shat aghts'an yem kerel.

282 - 3

I work in a factory.

Ես աշխատում եմ գործարանում:

Yes ashkhatum yem gortsaranum.

282 - 4

Just a moment.

Մեկ վայրկյան.

Mek vayrkyan.

282 - 5

I caught a cold.

Ես մրսեցի:

Yes mrsets'i.

282 - 6

It was my mistake.

Դա իմ սխալն էր:

Da im skhaln er.

41/52

282 - 7

I come from Chicago.

Ես գալիս եմ Չիկագոյից:

Yes galis yem Ch'ikagoyits'.

Day 282

Week 41

283 - 1

I got wet in the rain.

Ես թրջվեցի անձրևի տակ:

Yes t'rjvets'i andzrevi tak.

283 - 2

See you.

Կտեսնվենք.

Ktesnvenk'.

283 - 3

People speak French.

Մարդիկ խոսում են ֆրանսերեն:

Mardik khosum yen franseren:

283 - 4

I was the one to blame.

Ես էի մեղավորը:

Yes ei meghavory.

283 - 5

It's okay.

Ամեն ինչ կարգին է.

Amen inch' kargin e.

283 - 6

41/52

I don't have time.

Ես ժամանակ չունեմ:

Yes zhamanak ch'unem.

283 - 7

I'll go there by bus.

Ես ավտոբուսով կգնամ այնտեղ:

Yes avtobusov kgnam ayntegh.

Day 283

Week 41

284 - 1

Who knows the answer?

Ո՞վ գիտի պատասխանը։

VO՞v giti pataskhany.

284 - 2

Absolutely not.

Բացարձակապես ոչ։

Bats'ardzakapes voch':

284 - 3

Where have you been?

Որտեղ էիր?

Vortegh eir?

284 - 4

The dynamite exploded.

Դինամիտը պայթել է.

Dinamity payt'el e.

284 - 5

He burned his hand.

Նա այրեց ձեռքը։

Na ayrets' dzerrk'y

284 - 6

Have a nice weekend.

Հաճելի հանգստյան օր։

Hacheli hangstyan or:

41/52

284 - 7

Who's speaking?

Ո՞վ է խոսում։

VO՞v e khosum:

Day 284

Week 41

285 - 1

Did he attempt?

Փորձե՞լ է:

P'vordze°l e:

285 - 2

Complete the table.

Լրացրեք աղյուսակը:

Lrats'rek' aghyusaky:

285 - 3

I like you.

Ես հավանում եմ քեզ.

Yes havanum yem k'ez.

285 - 4

It's too loose.

Այն չափազանց ազատ է:

Ayn ch'ap'azants' azat e:

285 - 5

What will you do?

Ի՞նչ եք անելու:

I°nch' yek' anelu.

285 - 6

41/52

Blue is your colour!

Կապույտը քո գույնն է:

Kapuyty k'vo guynn e:

285 - 7

Judgment has been made.

Դատավճիռը կայացվել է.

Datavchirry kayats'vel e.

Day 285

Week 41

286 - 1

I broke my arm.

Ես կոտրեցի ձեռքս:

Yes kotrets'i dzerrk's.

286 - 2

Don't do such a thing.

Նման բան մի արեք:

Nman ban mi arek'.

286 - 3

I changed the sheets.

Ես փոխել եմ սավանները:

Yes p'vokhel yem savannery.

286 - 4

She is bleeding.

Նա արյունահոսում է:

Na aryunahosum e.

286 - 5

Where's the florist's?

Որտե՞ղ է ծաղկավաճառը:

Vorte°gh e tsaghkavacharry·

286 - 6

You deserve it!

Դու արժանի ես դրան!

Du arzhani yes dran!

286 - 7

We all saw him off.

Մենք բոլորս նրան ճանապարհեցինք:

Menk' bolors nran chanaparhets'ink'.

Day 286

Test 41

287 - 1

Where is the hospital?

287 - 2

I caught a cold.

287 - 3

I was the one to blame.

287 - 4

Where have you been?

287 - 5

Complete the table.

287 - 6

I broke my arm.

41/52

287 - 7

We all saw him off.

Day 287

Week 42

288 - 1

He suddenly disappeared.

Նա հանկարծ անհետացավ:

Na hankarts anhetats'av.

288 - 2

How is everybody?

Ինչպես են բոլորը:

Inch'pes yen bolory:

288 - 3

We got on the ship.

Մենք նավ նստեցինք:

Menk' nav nstets'ink'.

288 - 4

I'm not interested.

Ինձ չի հետաքրքրում.

Indz ch'i hetak'rk'rum.

288 - 5

He was shivering.

Նա դողում էր:

Na doghum ér,

288 - 6

I want to go shopping!

Ես ուզում եմ գնալ գնումներ!

Yes uzum yem gnal gnumner!

42/52

288 - 7

Would you like a bag?

Կցանկանայի՞ք պայուսակ:

Kts'ankanayi"k' payusak:

Day 288

Week 42

289 - 1

He denied the rumor.

Նա հերքեց այդ լուրերը.

Na herk'ets' ayd lurery.

289 - 2

I'll ride there.

Ես այնտեղ կք2եմ:

Yes ayntegh kk'shem.

289 - 3

I love stopovers.

Ես սիրում եմ կանգառներ:

Yes sirum yem kangarrner:

289 - 4

Ask him directly.

Հարցրեք նրան ուղղակիորեն:

Harts'rek' nran ughghakioren:

289 - 5

He is very smart.

Նա շատ խելացի է:

Na shat khelats'i e.

289 - 6

A coffee please.

Մի սուրճ խնդրում եմ:

Mi surch khndrum yem:

42/52

289 - 7

Is he your relative?

Նա քո ազգականն է:

Na k'vo azgakann e.

Day 289

Week 42

290 - 1

Happy Anniversary!

Շնորհավոր տարեդարձ!

Shnorhavor taredardz!

290 - 2

Sure, go ahead.

Իհարկե, շարունակիր:

Iharke, sharunakir:

290 - 3

Happy Birthday!

Ծնունդդ շնորհավոր!

Tsnundd shnorhavor!

290 - 4

I am ready.

Ես պատրաստ եմ.

Yes patrast yem.

290 - 5

I bought a new table.

Ես գնել եմ նոր սեղան:

Yes gnel yem nor seghan:

290 - 6

It's raining heavily.

Հորդառատ անձրև է գալիս:

Hordarrat andzrev e galis:

42/52

290 - 7

Time passes quickly.

Ժամանակն արագ է անցնում:

Zhamanakn arag e ants'num.

Day 290

Week 42

291 - 1

Do you have any quirks?

Դուք որևէ տարօրինակություններ ունե՞ք:

Duk' voreve tarorinakut'yunner une°k':

291 - 2

That's a great idea.

Դա հիանալի գաղափար է.

Da hianali gaghap'ar e.

291 - 3

Coffee is on the house.

Սուրճը տան վրա է:

Surchy tan vra e.

291 - 4

Please hold the door.

Խնդրում եմ, պահեք դուռը:

Khndrum yem, pahek' durry:

291 - 5

This seat is taken.

Այս նստատեղը գրավված է:

Ays nstateghy gravvats e:

291 - 6

Reduce the volume.

Կրճատել ձայնը:

Krchatel dzayny:

42/52

291 - 7

I don't fell well.

Ես լավ չեմ ընկել:

Yes lav ch'em ynkel:

Day 291

Week 42

292 - 1

I need a new toothbrush.

Ինձ նոր ատամի խոզանակ է պետք:

Indz nor atami khozanak e petk'.

292 - 2

He'll come after lunch.

Նա կգա ճաշից հետո:

Na kga chashits' heto:

292 - 3

How long will you wait?

Որքա՞ն ժամանակ եք սպասելու:

Vork'a"n zhamanak yek' spaselu:

292 - 4

Stop playing pranks.

Դադարեք կատակ խաղալը.

Dadarek' katak khaghaly.

292 - 5

It's an industrial city.

Արդյունաբերական քաղաք է:

Ardyunaberakan k'aghak' e

292 - 6

Talk to a witness.

Խոսեք վկայի հետ.

Khosek' vkayi het.

42/52

292 - 7

His wife is beautiful.

Նրա կինը գեղեցիկ է:

Nra kiny geghets'ik e.

Day 292

Week 42

293 - 1

Did you have breakfast?

Դուք նախաճաշե՞լ եք:

Duk' nakhachashe"l yek':

293 - 2

Please hold on.

Խնդրում եմ սպասիր.

Khndrum yem spasir.

293 - 3

How long will you stay?

Որքա՞ն ժամանակ եք մնալու:

Vork'a"n zhamanak yek' mnalu:

293 - 4

I'm glad to see you.

Ուրախ եմ քեզ տեսնելու համար:

Urakh yem k'ez tesnelu hamar:

293 - 5

It is quite tasty.

Այն բավականին համեղ է:

Ayn bavakanin hamegh e.

293 - 6

I'm not sure about it.

Ես դրանում վստահ չեմ:

Yes dranum vstah ch'em:

42/52

293 - 7

I couldn't agree more.

Ավելի շատ համաձայնել չէի կարող:

Aveli shat hamadzaynel ch'ei karogh.

Day 293

Test 42

294 - 1

I want to go shopping!

294 - 2

He is very smart.

294 - 3

I am ready.

294 - 4

Coffee is on the house.

294 - 5

He'll come after lunch.

294 - 6

Did you have breakfast?

42/52

294 - 7

I couldn't agree more.

Day 294

Week 43

295 - 1

My card has been stolen.
Իմ քարտը գողացել են.

Im k'arty goghats'el yen.

295 - 2

Great, thanks.
Հիանալի, շնորհակալություն:

Hianali, shnorhakalut'yun:

295 - 3

Did you call me?
Դուք ինձ զանգե՞լ եք:

Duk' indz zange°l yek':

295 - 4

How do I know that?
Ինչպե՞ս ես դա իմանամ:

Inch'pe°s yes da imanam:

295 - 5

May I have your address?
Կարո՞ղ եմ ունենալ ձեր հասցեն:

Karo°gh yem unenal dzer hasts'en:

295 - 6

43/52

I feel shy.
Ես ինձ ամաչկոտ եմ զգում:

Yes indz amach'kot yem zgum.

295 - 7

Pedestrian bridge.
Հետիոտնային կամուրջ.

Hetiotnayin kamurj.

Day 295

Week 43

296 - 1

How are your grades?

Ինչպե՞ս են գնահատականներդ:

Inch'pe°s yen gnahatakannerd:

296 - 2

He broke his promise.

Նա դրժեց իր խոստումը.

Na drzhets' ir khostumy.

296 - 3

I feel a little sad.

Ես մի փոքր տխուր եմ զգում:

Yes mi p'vok'r tkhur yem zgum:

296 - 4

What time does it start?

Որ ժամին է այն սկսվում?

Vor zhamin e ayn sksvum?

296 - 5

I have my own doubts.

Ես ունեմ իմ սեփական կասկածները.

Yes unem im sep'akan kaskatsnery

296 - 6

I run my own business.

Ես իմ սեփական բիզնեսն եմ վարում:

Yes im sep'akan biznesn yem varum.

43/52

296 - 7

I left her a message.

Ես նրան հաղորդագրություն եմ թողել:

Yes nran haghordagrut'yun yem t'voghel.

Day 296

Week 43

297 - 1

How long is the film?
Որքա՞ն է տևում ֆիլմը:
Vork'a°n e tevum filmy:

297 - 2

She was quiet at first.
Նա սկզբում լուռ էր:
Na skzbum lurr er:

297 - 3

Better luck next time.
Ավելի լավ հաջողություն հաջորդ անգամ:
Aveli lav hajoghut'yun hajord angam:

297 - 4

Is he a teacher?
Նա ուսուցի՞չ է:
Na usuts'i°ch' e.

297 - 5

It's five to five.
Հինգից հինգն է:
Hingits' hingn e:

297 - 6

I feel happy.
Ես երջանիկ եմ զգում.
Yes yerjanik yem zgum.

43/52

297 - 7

Is he binding a book?
Նա գիրք է կապում:
Na girk' e kapum:

Day 297

Week 43

298 - 1

I have no change.

Ես փոփոխություն չունեմ։

Yes p'vop'vokhut'yun ch'unem.

298 - 2

Please be seated.

Խնդրում եմ նստեք:

Khndrum yem nstek'.

298 - 3

I think you're right.

Կարծում եմ՝ դու ճիշտ ես:

Kartsum yem՝ du chisht yes.

298 - 4

Sounds great.

Հոյակապ է հնչում.

Hoyakap e hnch'um.

298 - 5

A full glass of milk.

Լրիվ բաժակ կաթ:

Lriv bazhak kat'

298 - 6

He is badly injured.

Նա ծանր վնասվածք է ստացել:

Na tsanr vnasvatsk' e stats'el.

43/52

298 - 7

He turned on the tap.

Նա բացեց ծորակը:

Na bats'ets' tsoraky.

Day 298

Week 43

299 - 1

I have a half-sister.

Ես ունեմ խորթ քույր:

Yes unem khort' k'uyr:

299 - 2

He came to my office.

Նա եկավ իմ գրասենյակ:

Na yekav im grasenyak.

299 - 3

This is my dream job.

Սա իմ երազանքի աշխատանքն է:

Sa im yerazank'i ashkhatank'n e.

299 - 4

He apologized at once.

Նա միանգամից ներողություն խնդրեց:

Na miangamits' neroghut'yun khndrets'.

299 - 5

I like oranges.

Նարինջ եմ սիրում:

Narinj yem sirum.

299 - 6

How sure are you?

Որքանո՞վ եք վստահ:

Vork'ano˝v yek' vstah:

43/52

299 - 7

I am a social worker.

Ես սոցիալական աշխատող եմ:

Yes sots'ialakan ashkhatogh yem.

Day 299

Week 43

300 - 1

I don't feel like it.

Ես դա չեմ զգում։

Yes da ch'em zgum:

300 - 2

The house is big.

Տունը մեծ է։

Tuny mets e.

300 - 3

I tend to think that.

Ես հակված եմ այդպես մտածել.

Yes hakvats yem aydpes mtatsel.

300 - 4

Heat the pan.

Տաքացրեք տապակը։

Tak'ats'rek' tapaky.

300 - 5

Listen to me.

Լսիր ինձ.

Lsir indz.

300 - 6

Put on your slippers!

Հագե՛ք ձեր հողաթափերը։

Hage'k' dzer hoghat'ap'ery.

300 - 7

She cried out for help.

Նա աղաղակեց օգնության համար։

Na aghaghakets' ognut'yan hamar:

Day 300

Test 43

301 - 1

I feel shy.

301 - 2

I have my own doubts.

301 - 3

Is he a teacher?

301 - 4

I think you're right.

301 - 5

He came to my office.

301 - 6

I don't feel like it.

43/52

301 - 7

She cried out for help.

Day 301

Week 44

302 - 1

This bra is too small.

Այս կրծկալը չափազանց փոքր է:

Ays krtskaly ch'ap'azants' p'vok'r e:

302 - 2

I think so, too.

Ես էլ եմ այդպես կարծում.

Yes el yem aydpes kartsum.

302 - 3

I have little money.

Ես քիչ փող ունեմ:

Yes k'ich' p'vogh unem.

302 - 4

Get lost.

Կորէլ.

Korel.

302 - 5

Stop talking, please.

Դադարիր խոսել, խնդրում եմ:

Dadarir khosel, khndrum yem

302 - 6

I am happy today.

Ես երջանիկ եմ այսօր:

Yes yerjanik yem aysor.

44/52

302 - 7

I work at a bank.

Ես աշխատում եմ բանկում:

Yes ashkhatum yem bankum:

Day 302

Week 44

303 - 1

The bath was lukewarm.

Լոգանքը գոլ էր:

Logank'y gol er.

303 - 2

Is it good for me?

Արդյո՞ք դա լավ է ինձ համար:

Ardyo"k' da lav e indz hamar:

303 - 3

I had twin baby girls.

Ես ունեի երկվորյակ աղջիկներ:

Yes unev yerkvoryak aghjikner:

303 - 4

I put butter in curry.

Կարրիի մեջ կարագ եմ լցրել:

Karrii mej karag yem lts'rel.

303 - 5

My nails have grown.

Եղունգներս մեծացել են:

Yeghungners metsats'el yen.

303 - 6

I hate ironing.

Ես ատում եմ արդուկելը:

Yes atum yem ardukely:

44/52

303 - 7

Please sign here.

Խնդրում ենք ստորագրել այստեղ:

Khndrum yenk' storagrel aystegh.

Day 303

Week 44

304 - 1

Don't waste my time.

Մի վատնեք իմ ժամանակը:

Mi vatnek' im zhamanaky:

304 - 2

I'll pay by card.

Ես կվճարեմ քարտով:

Yes kvcharem k'artov:

304 - 3

Long time no see.

Վաղուց չենք տեսնվել.

Vaghuts' ch'enk' tesnvel.

304 - 4

My father drives safely.

Հայրս ապահով քշում է:

Hayrs apahov k'shum e.

304 - 5

Stop making excuses.

Դադարեք արդարացումներ անել:

Dadarek' ardarats'umner anel·

304 - 6

I feel dizzy.

Ես զգում եմ գլխապտույտ.

Yes zgum yem glkhaptuyt.

44/52

304 - 7

He had indigestion.

Նա ուներ մարսողության խանգարում:

Na uner marsoghut'yan khangarum.

Day 304

Week 44

305 - 1

I am nervous.
Ես նյարդայնանում եմ.
Yes nyardaynanum yem.

305 - 2

His fingers are big.
Նրա մատները մեծ են:
Nra matnery mets yen.

305 - 3

Be quiet as you leave.
Հանգիստ եղիր հեռանալիս:
Hangist yeghir herranalis:

305 - 4

My pleasure.
Հաճույքով.
Hachuyk'ov.

305 - 5

I really like you.
Ես իրոք հավանում եմ քեզ.
Yes irok' havanum yem k'ez.

305 - 6

She is my grandmother.
Նա իմ տատիկն է:
Na im tatikn e.

44/52

305 - 7

How will you manage?
Ինչպե՞ս կհասցնեք:
Inch'pe˝s khasts'nek':

Day 305

Week 44

306 - 1

My teeth are strong.

Ատամներս ամուր են:

Atamners amur yen.

306 - 2

Is he learning English?

Նա սովորում է անգլերեն?

Na sovorum e angleren?

306 - 3

I unlaced my shoes.

Ես բացեցի կոշիկներս:

Yes bats'ets'i koshikners.

306 - 4

She was very brave.

Նա շատ համարձակ էր:

Na shat hamardzak er.

306 - 5

How do you go to office?

Ինչպե՞ս եք գնում գրասենյակ:

Inch'pe°s yek' gnum grasenyak·

306 - 6

Keep your word.

Պահիր քո խոսքը:

Pahir k'vo khosk'y.

44/52

306 - 7

I did my best.

Ես ամեն ինչ արեցի:

Yes amen inch' arets'i:

Day 306

Week 44

307 - 1

I see what you mean.

Ես հասկանում եմ, թե ինչ նկատի ունես:

Yes haskanum yem, t'e inch' nkati unes:

307 - 2

I live on my own.

Ես ապրում եմ ինքնուրույն:

Yes aprum yem ink'nuruyn:

307 - 3

Is he at home?

Նա տա՞նն է:

Na taˀnn e.

307 - 4

She has big legs.

Նա մեծ ոտքեր ունի:

Na mets votk'er uni:

307 - 5

I'm called John.

Ես կոչվում եմ Ջոն:

Yes koch'vum yem Jon:

307 - 6

He spoke loudly.

Նա բարձրաձայն խոսեց.

Na bardzradzayn khosets'.

307 - 7

I ate heartily.

Ես սրտանց կերա:

Yes srtants' kera.

Day 307

Test 44

308 - 1

I am happy today.

308 - 2

My nails have grown.

308 - 3

My father drives safely.

308 - 4

Be quiet as you leave.

308 - 5

Is he learning English?

308 - 6

I see what you mean.

44/52

308 - 7

I ate heartily.

Day 308

Week 45

309 - 1

Don't go there.

Մի գնա այնտեղ:

Mi gna ayntegh:

309 - 2

She's tall.

Նա բարձրահասակ է:

Na bardzrahasak e:

309 - 3

He was greatly pleased.

Նա շատ գոհ էր:

Na shat goh er.

309 - 4

Can I try it on, please?

Կարող եմ փորձել, խնդրում եմ:

Karogh yem p'vordzel, khndrum yem:

309 - 5

He is my best friend.

Նա իմ լավագույն ընկերն է.

Na im lavaguyn ynkern e.

309 - 6

It's very cool today.

Այսոր շատ զով է:

Aysor shat zov e:

45/52

309 - 7

The rear seat is empty.

Հետևի նստատեղը դատարկ է:

Hetevi nstateghy datark e.

Day 309

Week 45

310 - 1

First, you.

Նախ՝ դու:

Nakh` du.

310 - 2

He's quit smoking now.

Այժմ նա թողել է ծխելը:

Ayzhm na t'voghel e tskhely:

310 - 3

How is your husband?

Ինչպե՞ս է ամուսինդ:

Inch'pe˚s e amusind.

310 - 4

She ironed the shirt.

Նա արդուկեց վերնաշապիկը:

Na ardukets' vernashapiky:

310 - 5

Let's go home together.

Եկեք միասին գնանք տուն:

Yekek' miasin gnank' tun.

310 - 6

What's going on?

Ինչ է կատարվում?

Inch' e katarvum?

45/52

310 - 7

It's windy.

Քամոտ է.

K'amot e.

Day 310

Week 45

311 - 1

Where are you from?

Որտեղից ես?

Vorteghits' yes?

311 - 2

He works out every day.

Նա ամեն օր մարզվում է:

Na amen or marzvum e:

311 - 3

He's a great scholar.

Նա մեծ գիտնական է:

Na mets gitnakan e:

311 - 4

Did you listen to me?

Լսեցի՞ր ինձ:

Lsets'i'r indz.

311 - 5

My grandfather is well.

Պապս լավ է:

Paps lav e.

311 - 6

What is your shoe size?

Ո՞րն է ձեր կոշիկի չափը:

VO"rn e dzer koshiki ch'ap'y:

45/52

311 - 7

I keep my books here.

Ես իմ գրքերն այստեղ եմ պահում:

Yes im grk'ern aystegh yem pahum.

Day 311

Week 45

312 - 1

I like thin pillows.
Ես սիրում եմ բարակ բարձեր:
Yes sirum yem barak bardzer.

312 - 2

This is a real diamond.
Սա իսկական ադամանդ է:
Sa iskakan adamand e.

312 - 3

Don't shout.
Մի գոռացեք.
Mi gorrats'ek'.

312 - 4

My friend defended me.
Ընկերս պաշտպանեց ինձ:
Ynkers pashtpanets' indz.

312 - 5

It's too long.
Դա չափազանց երկար է:
Da ch'ap'azants' yerkar e:

312 - 6

Don't act recklessly.
Մի վարվեք անխոհեմ:
Mi varvek' ankhohem:

45/52

312 - 7

A slice of pizza.
Մի կտոր պիցցա.
Mi ktor pits'ts'a.

Day 312

Week 45

313 - 1

I'm okay. Thank you.

Ես լավ եմ. Շնորհակալություն.

Yes lav yem. Shnorhakalut'yun.

313 - 2

That's all right.

Ոչինչ:

Voch'inch':

313 - 3

Go ahead.

Շարունակիր.

Sharunakir.

313 - 4

I go to school by train.

Դպրոց եմ գնում գնացքով:

Dprots' yem gnum gnats'k'ov.

313 - 5

Next is your turn.

Հաջորդը ձեր հերթն է:

Hajordy dzer hert'n e:

313 - 6

Are you free now?

Դուք հիմա ազատ եք:

Duk' hima azat yek':

313 - 7

Why is the train late?

Ինչու՞ է գնացքն ուշանում.

Inch'u° e gnats'k'n ushanum.

Day 313

Week 45

314 - 1

Which one is the sauce?

Ո՞րն է սոուսը:

VO°rn e sousy:

314 - 2

I like a darker one.

Ինձ դուր է գալիս ավելի մուգը:

Indz dur e galis aveli mugy:

314 - 3

Don't worry.

Մի անհանգստացեք:

Mi anhangstats'ek':

314 - 4

I sorted out my clothes.

Հագուստս դասավորեցի:

Hagusts dasavorets'i.

314 - 5

I feel sleepy.

Քնաթաթախ եմ.

K'nat'at'akh yem.

314 - 6

I do not like you.

Դու ինձ դուր չես գալիս.

Du indz dur ch'es galis.

45/52

314 - 7

How did you reach there?

Ինչպե՞ս հասաք այնտեղ:

Inch'pe°s hasak' ayntegh:

Day 314

Test 45

315 - 1

It's very cool today.

315 - 2

Let's go home together.

315 - 3

Did you listen to me?

315 - 4

Don't shout.

315 - 5

That's all right.

315 - 6

Which one is the sauce?

315 - 7

How did you reach there?

Day 315

Week 46

316 - 1

The floor is wet.

Հատակը թաց է:

Hataky t'ats' e.

316 - 2

I don't understand why.

Չեմ հասկանում, թե ինչու:

CH'em haskanum, t'e inch'u.

316 - 3

I wouldn't mind.

Ես դեմ չէի լինի:

Yes dem ch'ei lini.

316 - 4

What did you do?

Ինչ արեցիր?

Inch' arets'ir?

316 - 5

He led her in the dance.

Նա առաջնորդեց նրան պարի մեջ:

Na arrajnordets' nran pari mej:

316 - 6

That's so kind of you.

Դա այնքան բարի է քո կողմից:

Da aynk'an bari e k'vo koghmits':

46/52

316 - 7

Are you awake?

Դուք արթուն եք

Duk' art'un yek'

Day 316

Week 46

317 - 1

Nice day, isn't it?
Հաճելի օր, այնպես չէ՞:
Hacheli or, aynpes ch'e°:

317 - 2

I bought a red rose.
Ես գնել եմ կարմիր վարդ:
Yes gnel yem karmir vard:

317 - 3

Slow down.
Դանդաղեցրեք.
Dandaghets'rek'.

317 - 4

We've run out of time.
Ժամանակը սպառվել է:
Zhamanaky sparrvel e:

317 - 5

Will they come here?
Նրանք կգա՞ն այստեղ:
Nrank' kga°n aystegh.

317 - 6

She has good manners.
Նա լավ վարք ունի:
Na lav vark' uni:

317 - 7

Come again?
Կրկին համեցեք?
Krkin hamets'ek'?

Day 317

Week 46

318 - 1

No passing.

Անցում չկա:

Ants'um ch'ka:

318 - 2

Who else wants to try?

Էլ ո՞վ է ուզում փորձել:

El vo°v e uzum p'vordzel:

318 - 3

It's very kind of you.

Շատ բարի է քո կողմից:

Shat bari e k'vo koghmits':

318 - 4

A woman approached me.

Ինձ մոտեցավ մի կին:

Indz motets'av mi kin.

318 - 5

Do you serve alcohol?

Դուք մատուցում եք ալկոհոլ:

Duk' matuts'um yek' alkohol·

318 - 6

It looks delicious.

Համեղ է երևում.

Hamegh e yerevum.

46/52

318 - 7

A sheet of pastry.

Մի թերթիկ խմորեղեն.

Mi t'ert'ik khmoreghen.

Day 318

Week 46

319 - 1

Yes, Sunday is fine.

Այո, կիրակի օրը լավ է:

Ayo, kiraki ory lav e:

319 - 2

Are you free next week?

Դուք ազատ եք հաջորդ շաբաթ:

Duk' azat yek' hajord shabat':

319 - 3

My wallet was stolen.

Դրամապանակս գողացել են.

Dramapanaks goghats'el yen.

319 - 4

I need a doctor.

Ինձ բժիշկ է պետք:

Indz bzhishk e petk'.

319 - 5

Do you sell swimsuits?

Դուք լողազգեստներ վաճառու՞մ եք:

Duk' loghazgestner vacharru˚m yek'.

319 - 6

I sealed the letter.

Ես կնքեցի նամակը:

Yes knk'ets'i namaky.

319 - 7

Make a withdrawal.

Կատարեք դուրսբերում:

Katarek' dursberum:

Day 319

Week 46

320 - 1

This apple's rotten.

Այս խնձորը փտած է:

Ays khndzory p'tats e:

320 - 2

My throat is a bit dry.

Կոկորդս մի քիչ չորացել է:

Kokords mi k'ich' ch'vorats'el e.

320 - 3

It's not true.

Դա չի համապատասխանում իրականությանը.

Da ch'i hamapataskhanum irakanut'yany.

320 - 4

I received a threat.

Ես սպառնալիք եմ ստացել.

Yes sparrnalik' yem stats'el.

320 - 5

The knife cuts well.

Դանակը լավ կտրում է:

Danaky lav ktrum e

320 - 6

I need some medicine.

Ինձ որոշ դեղամիջոց է պետք:

Indz vorosh deghamijots' e petk':

320 - 7

I've been tired today.

Ես այսոր հոգնած էի:

Yes aysor hognats ei:

46/52

Day 320

Week 46

321 - 1

I inhaled dust.

Ես փոշի եմ ներշնչել.

Yes p'voshi yem nershnch'el.

321 - 2

That is 100% cotton.

Դա 100% բամբակ է:

Da 100% bambak e.

321 - 3

I dried the wet clothes.

Ես չորացրեցի թաց շորերը:

Yes ch'vorats'rets'i t'ats' shorery.

321 - 4

The light is still on.

Լույսը դեռ վառվում է:

Luysy derr varrvum e.

321 - 5

I love dogs.

Ես սիրում եմ շներին:

Yes sirum yem shnerin:

321 - 6

Your name please?

Ձեր անունը խնդրում եմ:

DZer anuny khndrum yem:

321 - 7

Do me a favor.

Ինձ լավություն արա.

Indz lavut'yun ara.

Day 321

Test 46

322 - 1

That's so kind of you.

322 - 2

Will they come here?

322 - 3

A woman approached me.

322 - 4

My wallet was stolen.

322 - 5

My throat is a bit dry.

322 - 6

I inhaled dust.

322 - 7

46/52

Do me a favor.

Day 322

Week 47

323 - 1

Is this your bag?

Սա քո՞ պայուսակն է:

Sa k'vo° payusakn e:

323 - 2

He's a famous singer.

Նա հայտնի երգիչ է:

Na haytni yergich' e.

323 - 3

What a beautiful sunset!

Ի՜նչ գեղեցիկ մայրամուտ:

I˜nch' geghets'ik mayramut.

323 - 4

You were almost right.

Դուք գրեթե ճիշտ էիք:

Duk' gret'e chisht eik':

323 - 5

I love my family.

Ես սիրում եմ իմ ընտանիքը.

Yes sirum yem im yntanik'y.

323 - 6

I'm studying Japanese.

Ես սովորում եմ ճապոներեն:

Yes sovorum yem chaponeren.

323 - 7

Sorry to say that.

Կներեք դա ասելու համար:

Knerek' da aselu hamar:

Day 323

Week 47

324 - 1

How much is it?

Ինչ արժե՞

Inch' arzhe?

324 - 2

What street is this?

Սա ի՞նչ փողոց է:

Sa i"nch' p'voghots' e.

324 - 3

You are so kind.

Դուք շատ բարի եք.

Duk' shat bari yek'.

324 - 4

Pretty well.

Շատ լավ:

Shat lav:

324 - 5

How do you manage?

Ինչպե՞ս եք կարողանում:

Inch'pe"s yek' karoghanum·

324 - 6

Please pay in cash.

Խնդրում ենք վճարել կանխիկ:

Khndrum yenk' vcharel kankhik:

324 - 7

47/52

Congratulations!

Շնորհավորում եմ:

Shnorhavorum yem:

Day 324

Week 47

325 - 1

Her skin is smooth.

Նրա մաշկը հարթ է:

Nra mashky hart' e:

325 - 2

Focus on your goal.

Կենտրոնացեք ձեր նպատակի վրա:

Kentronats'ek' dzer npataki vra:

325 - 3

He is my classmate.

Նա իմ դասընկերն է:

Na im dasynkern e.

325 - 4

I chilled beer.

Ես սառեցրեցի գարեջուր:

Yes sarrets'rets'i garejur:

325 - 5

I'm not good at math.

Ես մաթեմատիկայից լավ չեմ:

Yes mat'ematikayits' lav ch'em:

325 - 6

I can do it.

Ես կարող եմ դա անել.

Yes karogh yem da anel.

47/52

325 - 7

Don't tell lies.

Սուտ մի ասա.

Sut mi asa.

Day 325

Week 47

326 - 1

Show me our sales.

Ցույց տվեք մեր վաճառքները։

Ts'uyts' tvek' mer vacharrk'nery:

326 - 2

That is common sense.

Դա ողջախոհություն է։

Da voghjakhohut'yun e:

326 - 3

Do not move the victim.

Մի շարժեք տուժածին.

Mi sharzhek' tuzhatsin.

326 - 4

I doubt it.

Ես կասկածում եմ.

Yes kaskatsum yem.

326 - 5

Do you work on Sundays?

Դուք աշխատում եք կիրակի օրերին։

Duk' ashkhatum yek' kiraki orerin:

326 - 6

Does he beat me?

Նա ծեծու՞մ է ինձ։

Na tsetsu"m e indz.

326 - 7

I didn't wake up early.

Ես շուտ չէի արթնացել։

Yes shut ch'ei art'nats'el.

47/52

Day 326

Week 47

327 - 1

Let's order first.
Եկեք նախ պատվիրենք.
Yekek' nakh patvirenk'.

327 - 2

I moved last year.
Ես տեղափոխվել եմ անցյալ տարի:
Yes teghap'vokhvel yem ants'yal tari:

327 - 3

I bought a leather belt.
Ես գնել եմ կաշվե գոտի:
Yes gnel yem kashve goti:

327 - 4

Just a minute please.
Խնդրում եմ ընդամենը մեկ րոպե:
Khndrum yem yndameny mek rope:

327 - 5

There's no other way.
Ուրիշ ճանապարհ չկա:
Urish chanaparh ch'ka.

327 - 6

You're so sweet.
Դուք այնքան քաղցր եք:
Duk' aynk'an k'aghts'r yek':

47/52

327 - 7

How did they escape?
Ինչպե՞ս են նրանք փախել:
Inch'pe°s yen nrank' p'akhel.

Day 327

Week 47

328 - 1

Do like your job?

Ձեզ դուր է գալիս ձեր աշխատանքը:

DZez dur e galis dzer ashkhatank'y:

328 - 2

The weather is hot.

Եղանակը շոգ է:

Yeghanaky shog e.

328 - 3

I am looking for a job.

Ես աշխատանք եմ փնտրում:

Yes ashkhatank' yem p'ntrum.

328 - 4

I am on a business trip.

Ես գործուղման եմ:

Yes gortsughman yem.

328 - 5

The house is spacious.

Տունը ընդարձակ է:

Tuny yndardzak e.

328 - 6

No, not at all.

Ոչ, ամենևին:

Voch', amenevin:

328 - 7

My head aches.

Գլուխս ցավում է:

Glukhs ts'avum e.

Day 328

Test 47

I'm studying Japanese.

How do you manage?

I chilled beer.

Do not move the victim.

I moved last year.

Do like your job?

My head aches.

Day 329

Week 48

330 - 1

He's very expressive.

Նա շատ արտահայտիչ է:

Na shat artahaytich' e:

330 - 2

I like to be alone.

Ես սիրում եմ մենակ լինել:

Yes sirum yem menak linel.

330 - 3

That is okay.

Դա նորմալ է:

Da normal e:

330 - 4

This blanket is warm.

Այս վերմակը տաք է:

Ays vermaky tak' e:

330 - 5

I want to get in shape.

Ուզում եմ մարզավիճակ ձեռք բերել:

Uzum yem marzavichak dzerrk' borol.

330 - 6

Where did he come?

Որտեղ է նա եկել:

Vortegh e na yekel:

330 - 7

Is he paying the fee?

Նա վճարու՞մ է վճարը:

Na vcharu˚m e vchary.

48/52

Day 330

Week 48

331 - 1

We are three sisters.

Մենք երեք քույր ենք:

Menk' yerek' k'uyr yenk'.

331 - 2

He lost his girlfriend.

Նա կորցրել է իր ընկերուհուն.

Na korts'rel e ir ynkeruhun.

331 - 3

I don't have work today.

Ես այսօր աշխատանք չունեմ.

Yes aysor ashkhatank' ch'unem.

331 - 4

My car is broken.

Իմ մեքենան կոտրվել է.

Im mek'enan kotrvel e.

331 - 5

When will he be back?

Ե՞րբ նա կվերադառնա:

Ye*rb na kveradarrna:

331 - 6

Is the machine working?

Մեքենան աշխատում է:

Mek'enan ashkhatum e:

331 - 7

Of course.

Իհարկե.

Iharke.

48/52

Day 331

Week 48

332 - 1

What are your symptoms?

Որո՞նք են ձեր ախտանիշները:

Voro°nk' yen dzer akhtanishnery:

332 - 2

Is she going to Delhi?

Նա գնում է Դելի:

Na gnum e Deli:

332 - 3

Why do you worry?

Ինչո՞ւ եք անհանգստանում:

Inch'vo°w yek' anhangstanum.

332 - 4

I don't know yet.

Ես դեռ չգիտեմ:

Yes derr ch'gitem.

332 - 5

I need home insurance.

Ինձ տան ապահովագրություն է պետք:

Indz tan apahovagrut'yun e petk'.

332 - 6

It's nice out today.

Հաճելի է դուրս գալ այսօր:

Hacheli e durs gal aysor:

332 - 7

48/52

Do you have a black pen?

Դուք ունե՞ք սև գրիչ:

Duk' une°k' sev grich':

Day 332

Week 48

333 - 1

It's hot outside.

Դրսում շոգ է:

Drsum shog e.

333 - 2

He is a lucky man.

Նա բախտավոր մարդ է:

Na bakhtavor mard e.

333 - 3

Can you help me?

Կարող ես ինձ օգնել?

Karogh yes indz ognel?

333 - 4

Can I sit here?

Կարո՞ղ եմ այստեղ նստել:

Karo°gh yem aystegh nstel:

333 - 5

It's time for lunch.

Ճաշի ժամանակն է:

Chashi zhamanakn e.

333 - 6

He's learning karate.

Նա սովորում է կարատե:

Na sovorum e karate:

333 - 7

48/52

He has feelings for her.

Նա զգացմունքներ ունի նրա հանդեպ:

Na zgats'munk'ner uni nra handep:

Day 333

Week 48

334 - 1

Is the story real?

Արդյո՞ք պատմությունը իրական է:

Ardyo"k' patmut'yuny irakan e:

334 - 2

Please, come in.

Խնդրում եմ, ներս արի:

Khndrum yem, ners ari.

334 - 3

Are you on Facebook?

Ֆեյսբուքում ես?

Feysbuk'um yes?

334 - 4

This meat is not fresh.

Այս միսը թարմ չէ:

Ays misy t'arm ch'e.

334 - 5

Does the bomb blast?

Արդյո՞ք ռումբը պայթում է:

Ardyo"k' rrumby payt'um e.

334 - 6

Thanks for calling.

Շնորհակալություն զանգահարելու համար:

Shnorhakalut'yun zangaharelu hamar:

334 - 7

Where's the grocer's?

Որտե՞ղ է նպարեղենը:

Vorte"gh e nparegheny:

48/52

Day 334

Week 48

335 - 1

He owns three cars.

Նրան են պատկանում երեք ավտոմեքենա:

Nran yen patkanum yerek' avtomek'ena.

335 - 2

Happy Valentine's Day!

Շնորհավոր սուրբ Վալենտինի օրը!

Shnorrhavor surb Valentini ory!

335 - 3

I saw the trailer.

Ես տեսա թրեյլերը:

Yes tesa t'reylery.

335 - 4

She's greedy.

Նա ագահ է:

Na agah e:

335 - 5

Is he breathing?

Նա շնչու՞մ է:

Na shnch'u˚m e.

335 - 6

What turns you on?

Ի՞նչն է ձեզ միացնում:

I˚nch'n e dzez miats'num:

335 - 7

48/52

Is he coming regularly?

Նա պարբերաբար գալիս է?

Na parberabar galis e?

Day 335

Test 48

336 - 1

Where did he come?

336 - 2

When will he be back?

336 - 3

I don't know yet.

336 - 4

Can you help me?

336 - 5

Please, come in.

336 - 6

He owns three cars.

336 - 7

Is he coming regularly?

48/52

Day 336

Week 49

337 - 1

Jump at the chance.

Անցնել հնարավորության դեպքում:

Ants'nel hnaravorut'yan depk'um:

337 - 2

What was your best trip?

Ո՞րն էր ձեր լավագույն ճամփորդությունը:

VO"rn er dzer lavaguyn champ'vordut'yuny:

337 - 3

Don't worry about it.

Մի անհանգստացեք դրա մասին:

Mi anhangstats'ek' dra masin:

337 - 4

I have one brother.

Ես ունեմ մեկ եղբայր.

Yes unem mek yeghbayr.

337 - 5

Let me pour you a drink.

Թույլ տվեք ձեզ խմել:

T'uyl tvek' dzez khmel:

337 - 6

This is a danger zone.

Սա վտանգավոր գոտի է:

Sa vtangavor goti e.

337 - 7

49/52

Please show me.

Խնդրում եմ ցույց տուր ինձ:

Khndrum yem ts'uyts' tur indz.

Day 337

Week 49

338 - 1

She hasn't noticed me.
Նա ինձ չի նկատել:
Na indz ch'i nkatel:

338 - 2

He's still single.
Նա դեռ միայնակ է:
Na derr miaynak e:

338 - 3

We met yesterday.
Երեկ հանդիպեցինք:
Yerek handipets'ink'.

338 - 4

It's half past eleven.
Ժամը տասնմեկ անց կես է:
Zhamy tasnmek ants' kes e.

338 - 5

I'll connect you now.
Ես քեզ հիմա միացնեմ:
Yes k'ez hima miats'nem:

338 - 6

This smells too sweet.
Սա չափազանց քաղցր հոտ է գալիս:
Sa ch'ap'azants' k'aghts'r hot e galis:

338 - 7

There's a sample here.
Այստեղ կա նմուշ:
Aystegh ka nmush:

49/52

Day 338

Week 49

339 - 1

My stomach hurts a lot.

Ստամոքս շատ է ցավում:

Stamok's shat e ts'avum.

339 - 2

How much does it cost?

Որքա՞ն արժե այն:

Vork'a"n arzhe ayn:

339 - 3

Don't make noise.

Աղմուկ մի՛ հանիր:

Aghmuk mi˙ hanir.

339 - 4

My trousers got dirty.

Տաբատս կեղտոտվեց:

Tabats keghtotvets'.

339 - 5

Mind your business.

Ուշադրություն դարձրեք ձեր գործին:

Ushadrut'yun dardzrek' dzer gortsin:

339 - 6

I like dogs.

Ես սիրում եմ շներ:

Yes sirum yem shner:

339 - 7

I called the waitress.

Զանգեցի մատուցողուհուն:

Zangets'i matuts'voghuhun.

49/52

Day 339

Week 49

340 - 1

Can you speak English?

Կարող ես խոսել անգլերեն?

Karogh yes khosel angleren?

340 - 2

It's very cheap.

Շատ էժան է:

Shat ezhan e.

340 - 3

He injured his elbow.

Նա վնասել է արմունկը:

Na vnasel e armunky.

340 - 4

Fantastic.

Ֆանտաստիկ.

Fantastik.

340 - 5

She gripped my hand.

Նա բռնեց իմ ձեռքը:

Na hrrnetc' im drerrk'y.

340 - 6

Just stay focused.

Պարզապես մնա կենտրոնացած:

Parzapes mna kentronats'ats:

340 - 7

The view is incredible.

Տեսարանը անհավանական է:

Tesarany anhavanakan e.

49/52

Day 340

Week 49

341 - 1

It's a fair way away.

Դա բավականին հեռու է:

Da bavakanin herru e:

341 - 2

The skirt is too short.

Կիսաշրջազգեստը չափազանց կարճ է:

Kisashrjazgesty ch'ap'azants' karch e.

341 - 3

What is your opinion?

Ինչ է ձեր կարծիքը?

Inch' e dzer kartsik'y?

341 - 4

I need to see a doctor.

Ես պետք է բժիշկ տեսնեմ:

Yes petk' e bzhishk tesnem:

341 - 5

He joined our team.

Նա միացավ մեր թիմին:

Na miats'av mer t'imin.

341 - 6

I sold old books.

Ես հին գրքեր էի վաճառում:

Yes hin grk'er ei vacharrum.

341 - 7

Stop fighting.

Դադարեցրեք պայքարը.

Dadarets'rek' payk'ary.

49/52

Day 341

Week 49

342 - 1

I have no choice.

Ես այլընտրանք չունեմ:

Yes aylyntrank' ch'unem.

342 - 2

Do not wash.

Մի լվացեք:

Mi lvats'ek':

342 - 3

Happy Holidays!

Ուրախ արձակուրդ!

Urakh ardzakurd!

342 - 4

Let me introduce myself.

Թույլ տվեք ներկայանալ.

T'uyl tvek' nerkayanal.

342 - 5

He is motivated to work.

Նա մոտիվացված է աշխատելու:

Na motivats'vats e ashkhatelu.

342 - 6

He is a dentist.

Նա ատամնաբույժ է:

Na atamnabuyzh e.

342 - 7

Please feel free.

Խնդրում եմ ազատ զգալ:

Khndrum yem azat zgal:

49/52

Day 342

Test 49

343 - 1

This is a danger zone.

343 - 2

I'll connect you now.

343 - 3

My trousers got dirty.

343 - 4

He injured his elbow.

343 - 5

The skirt is too short.

343 - 6

I have no choice.

343 - 7

Please feel free.

49/52

Day 343

Week 50

344 - 1

The battery is flat.

Մարտկոցը լիցքաթափված է:

Martkots'y lits'k'at'ap'vats e.

344 - 2

I have the flu.

Ես գրիպ ունեմ:

Yes grip unem.

344 - 3

We will have a meeting.

Մենք հանդիպում կունենանք:

Menk' handipum kunenank'.

344 - 4

Oh no, what a shame.

О, ոչ, ինչ ամոթ է:

O, voch', inch' amot' e:

344 - 5

I have no money.

Ես փող չունեմ:

Yes p'vogh ch'unem.

344 - 6

He is unconscious.

Նա անգիտակից վիճակում է:

Na angitakits' vichakum e.

344 - 7

He is hungry.

Նա քաղցած է.

Na k'aghts'ats e.

50/52

Day 344

Week 50

345 - 1

I left a key with him.

Ես նրա մոտ բանալի թողեցի:

Yes nra mot banali t'voghets'i.

345 - 2

My grandfather got sick.

Պապս հիվանդացավ:

Paps hivandats'av.

345 - 3

Best of luck.

Լավագույն հաջողություն:

Lavaguyn hajoghut'yun:

345 - 4

I have a stomachache.

Ես ստամոքսի ցավ ունեմ:

Yes stamok'si ts'av unem.

345 - 5

Are you sure?

Համոզված ես?

Hamozvats yes?

345 - 6

I paid my car tax.

Ես վճարել եմ իմ մեքենայի հարկը.

Yes vcharel yem im mek'enayi harky.

345 - 7

Do you understand?

Դու հասկանում ես?

Du haskanum yes?

50/52

Day 345

Week 50

346 - 1

Cross the street.

Անցնել փողոցը.

Ants'nel p'voghots'y.

346 - 2

Where is the exit?

Որտե՞ղ է ելքը:

Vorte°gh e yelk'y:

346 - 3

It's too long for me.

Ինձ համար դա չափազանց երկար է:

Indz hamar da ch'ap'azants' yerkar e:

346 - 4

Where does he live?

Որտեղ է նա ապրում?

Vortegh e na aprum?

346 - 5

Many happy returns.

Շատ երջանիկ վերադարձներ:

Shat yerjanik vordardzner.

346 - 6

Time went by so fast.

Ժամանակն այնքան արագ անցավ:

Zhamanakn aynk'an arag ants'av.

346 - 7

When did he come?

Ե՞րբ է նա եկել:

Ye°rb e na yekel.

50/52

Day 346

Week 50

347 - 1

Let's call the waiter.

Եկեք զանգենք մատուցողին:

Yekek' zangenk' matuts'voghin.

347 - 2

He is not a bad person.

Նա վատ մարդ չէ:

Na vat mard ch'e.

347 - 3

Your sister is kind.

Քույրդ բարի է:

K'uyrd bari e.

347 - 4

I'm physically strong.

Ես ֆիզիկապես ուժեղ եմ.

Yes fizikapes uzhegh yem.

347 - 5

In what price range?

Ինչ գնային միջակայքում:

Inch' gnayin mijakayk'um:

347 - 6

How about three o'clock?

Իսկ ի՞նչ կասեք ժամը երեքի մասին:

Isk i°nch' kasek' zhamy yerek'i masin.

347 - 7

Here's my ID.

Ահա իմ ID-ն:

Aha im ID-n:

50/52

Day 347

Week 50

348 - 1

I eat bread every day.

Ես ամեն օր հաց եմ ուտում։

Yes amen or hats' yem utum.

348 - 2

Did you enjoy the meal?

Դուք վայելե՞լ եք ճաշը։

Duk' vayele°l yek' chashy:

348 - 3

The pain is too much.

Ցավը չափազանց շատ է։

Ts'avy ch'ap'azants' shat e.

348 - 4

What is your dress size?

Ո՞րն է ձեր զգեստի չափը։

VO°rn e dzer zgesti ch'ap'y:

348 - 5

Sunglasses suit him.

Նրան սազում են արևային ակնոցները։

Nran sazum yen arevnyin aknots'nery.

348 - 6

Take a look around.

Նայիր շուրջը.

Nayir shurjy.

348 - 7

Does he befit always?

Արդյո՞ք նա հարիր է միշտ։

Ardyo°k' na harir e misht:

50/52

Day 348

Week 50

349 - 1

I have no office today.

Ես այսօր գրասենյակ չունեմ:

Yes aysor grasenyak ch'unem.

349 - 2

Does the sun appear?

Արևը հայտնվում է?

Arevy haytnvum e?

349 - 3

Do you hate him?

Դուք ատո՞ւմ եք նրան:

Duk' ato°wm yek' nran.

349 - 4

Find the value of x.

Գտե՛ք x-ի արժեքը:

Gte k' x-i arzhek'y.

349 - 5

The boss is coming.

Բոսը գալիս է:

Bosy galis e.

349 - 6

It's very near.

Շատ մոտ է:

Shat mot e.

349 - 7

Where do I come from?

Որտեղի՞ց եմ ես գալիս:

Vorteghi°ts' yem yes galis.

50/52

Day 349

Test 50

350 - 1

He is unconscious.

350 - 2

Are you sure?

350 - 3

Where does he live?

350 - 4

Your sister is kind.

350 - 5

Did you enjoy the meal?

350 - 6

I have no office today.

350 - 7

Where do I come from?

50/52

Day 350

Week 51

351 - 1

Do whatever you want.

Արա ինչ ուզում ես:

Ara inch' uzum yes.

351 - 2

Here is the bill.

Ահա օրինագիծը.

Aha orinagitsy.

351 - 3

A fly is buzzing.

Մի ճանճ է բզզում:

Mi chanch e bzzum.

351 - 4

It's been so cold.

Այնքան ցուրտ է եղել:

Aynk'an ts'urt e yeghel:

351 - 5

The food here is bad.

Սնունդն այստեղ վատ է:

Snundn aystegh vat e.

351 - 6

No, that's not true.

Ոչ, դա ճիշտ չէ:

Voch', da chisht ch'e:

351 - 7

What is he?

Ինչ է նա?

Inch' e na?

51/52

Day 351

Week 51

352 - 1

Someone stole my bag.

Ինչ-որ մեկը գողացավ իմ պայուսակը.

Inch'-vor meky goghats'av im payusaky.

352 - 2

How is it?

Ինչպես է դա?

Inch'pes e da?

352 - 3

It's cloudy today.

Այսոր ամպամած է:

Aysor ampamats e.

352 - 4

The sky is deep blue.

Երկինքը մուգ կապույտ է:

Yerkink'y mug kapuyt e.

352 - 5

Is she reading a novel?

Նա վե՞պ է կարդում:

Na vo՞p e kardum.

352 - 6

How is this cooked?

Ինչպես է սա եփում:

Inch'pes e sa yep'um:

352 - 7

She's very honest.

Նա շատ ազնիվ է:

Na shat azniv e:

51/52

Day 352

Week 51

353 - 1

Nice to meet you too.
Հաճելի է հանդիպել Ձեզ նույնպես.

Hacheli e handipel DZez nuynpes.

353 - 2

What is my room number?
Ո՞րն է իմ սենյակի համարը:

VO"rn e im senyaki hamary:

353 - 3

Don't ask me anything.
Ինձ ոչինչ մի հարցրու:

Indz voch'inch' mi harts'ru.

353 - 4

She's a quiet person.
Նա հանգիստ մարդ է:

Na hangist mard e:

353 - 5

I work as a doctor.
Ես աշխատում եմ որպես բժիշկ:

Yes ashkhatum yem vorpes bzhishk.

353 - 6

My sister is kind.
Քույրս բարի է:

K'uyrs bari e.

353 - 7

He watches movies a lot.
Նա շատ է ֆիլմեր դիտում:

Na shat e filmer ditum.

51/52

Day 353

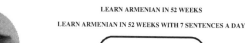

Week 51

354 - 1

Wear your life guards.

Հագեք ձեր փրկարարները:

Hagek' dzer p'rkararnery:

354 - 2

I don't understand.

Չեմ հասկանում:

CH'em haskanum.

354 - 3

No trespassing here.

Այստեղ ոտնձգություն չկա:

Aystegh votndzgut'yun ch'ka:

354 - 4

I looked up at the sky.

Ես նայեցի երկնքին:

Yes nayets'i yerknk'in.

354 - 5

He's acting strange.

Նա տարorինակ է վարվում:

Na tarorinak e varvum:

354 - 6

I'm in charge of sales.

Ես պատասխանատու եմ վաճառքի համար:

Yes pataskhanatu yem vacharrk'i hamar:

354 - 7

Take them with you.

Վերցրեք դրանք ձեզ հետ:

Verts'rek' drank' dzez het:

51/52

Day 354

Week 51

355 - 1

Here's the menu.

Ահա Ճաշացանկը:

Aha chashats'anky:

355 - 2

I understand.

Հասկանում եմ.

Haskanum yem.

355 - 3

It was a very sad movie.

Շատ տխուր ֆիլմ էր:

Shat tkhur film er.

355 - 4

Do not lie.

Մի ստիր.

Mi stir.

355 - 5

Have you been lifting?

Դուք բարձրացրե՞լ եք:

Duk' bardzrats're°l yek':

355 - 6

It's very cold outside.

Դրսում շատ ցուրտ է:

Drsum shat ts'urt e.

355 - 7

We have to work on it.

Մենք պետք է աշխատենք դրա վրա:

Menk' petk' e ashkhatenk' dra vra:

51/52

Day 355

Week 51

356 - 1

Did he come?

Եկե՞լ է:

Yeke"l e.

356 - 2

There is an explosion.

Պայթյուն է տեղի ունենում.

Payt'yun e teghi unenum.

356 - 3

Please call back later.

Խնդրում ենք հետ զանգահարել ավելի ուշ:

Khndrum yenk' het zangaharel aveli ush:

356 - 4

What is your occupation?

Ո՞րն է քո զբաղմունքը:

VO"rn e k'vo zbaghmunk'y:

356 - 5

How did you get there?

Ինչպես Դուք Գնացիք Այնտեղ?

Inch'pon Duk' Gnats'ik Ayntegh?

356 - 6

Dry your hair well.

Լավ չորացրեք ձեր մազերը:

Lav ch'vorats'rek' dzer mazery.

356 - 7

He is a radiographer.

Ռենտգենաբան է:

RRentgenaban e.

51/52

Day 356

Test 51

357 - 1

No, that's not true.

357 - 2

Is she reading a novel?

357 - 3

She's a quiet person.

357 - 4

No trespassing here.

357 - 5

I understand.

357 - 6

Did he come?

357 - 7

He is a radiographer.

51/52

Day 357

Week 52

358 - 1

What sizes do you have?

Ի՞նչ չափսեր ունեք:

I˚nch' ch'ap'ser unek':

358 - 2

Add a little more salt.

Մի քիչ էլ աղ ավելացրեք:

Mi k'ich' el agh avelats'rek'.

358 - 3

Do you have a stool?

Դուք ունե՞ք աթոռակ:

Duk' une˚k' at'vorrak:

358 - 4

Drink your coffee.

Խմեք ձեր սուրճը:

Khmek' dzer surchy:

358 - 5

I've got to go now.

Ես հիմա պետք է գնամ:

Yes himn petk' u gnam:

358 - 6

A leaf fluttered down.

Մի տերև թռավ ներքև:

Mi terev t'rrav nerk'ev.

358 - 7

I feel sad today.

Ես այսօր տխուր եմ զգում:

Yes aysor tkhur yem zgum:

52/52

Day 358

Week 52

359 - 1

Was I appointed?

Ես նշանակվե՞լ եմ:

Yes nshanakveˮl yem.

359 - 2

Is this show good?

Արդյո՞ք այս ներկայացումը լավն է:

Ardyoˮk' ays nerkayats'umy lavn e:

359 - 3

How have you been?

Ինչպե՞ս եք եղել:

Inch'peˮs yek' yeghel:

359 - 4

His house is very big.

Նրա տունը շատ մեծ է:

Nra tuny shat mets e.

359 - 5

Actually, I like her.

Իրականում, ինձ դուր է գալիս նա:

Irakanum, indz dur e galis na:

359 - 6

The meal is ready.

Ճաշը պատրաստ է:

Chashy patrast e.

359 - 7

Is that seat available?

Այդ նստատեղը հասանելի՞ է:

Ayd nstateghy hasaneliˮ e:

52/52

Day 359

Week 52

360 - 1

It's not a big deal.

Դա մեծ խնդիր չէ:

Da mets khndir ch'e:

360 - 2

Please come at once.

Խնդրում եմ միանգամից եկեք:

Khndrum yem miangamits' yekek'.

360 - 3

Incredible.

Անհավատալի.

Anhavatali.

360 - 4

It's going to rain.

Անձրև է գալու:

Andzrev e galu:

360 - 5

Look before you leap.

Նայեք նախքան ցատկելը:

Nayek' nakhk'an ts'atkely:

360 - 6

This bag is heavy.

Այս պայուսակը ծանր է:

Ays payusaky tsanr e:

360 - 7

Ice is a solid.

Սառույցը պինդ է:

Sarruyts'y pind e:

52/52

Day 360

Week 52

361 - 1

That pond is very deep.

Այդ լճակը շատ խորն է:

Ayd lchaky shat khorn e.

361 - 2

She sued the company.

Նա դատի է տվել ընկերությանը:

Na dati e tvel ynkerut'yany.

361 - 3

This bra is too large.

Այս կրծկալը չափազանց մեծ է:

Ays krtskaly ch'ap'azants' mets e:

361 - 4

I like wine.

Ես սիրում եմ գինի:

Yes sirum yem gini:

361 - 5

When do you return home?

Ե՞րբ եք վերադառնում տուն:

Ye°rb yek' veradarrnum tun:

361 - 6

I hate cigarettes.

Ես ատում եմ ծխախոտը:

Yes atum yem tskhakhoty:

361 - 7

Look up.

Փնտրել.

P'ntrel.

52/52

Day 361

Week 52

362 - 1

The bath is ready.
Լոգանքը պատրաստ է:

Logank'y patrast e.

362 - 2

Talk to you later.
Ավելի ուշ խոսեք ձեզ հետ:

Aveli ush khosek' dzez het:

362 - 3

Please move forward.
Խնդրում եմ առաջ շարժվեք:

Khndrum yem arraj sharzhvek':

362 - 4

That's an extreme idea.
Դա ծայրահեղ գաղափար է:

Da tsayrahegh gaghap'ar e:

362 - 5

He hit on a good idea.
Նա հարվածեց մի լավ գաղափարի:

Na harvatsets' mi lav gaghap'ari:

362 - 6

I'm a student.
Ես ուսանող եմ:

Yes usanogh yem.

362 - 7

What's the time?
Ժամը քանիսն է?

Zhamy k'anisn e?

52/52

Day 362

Week 52

363 - 1

It's too tight.

Այս չափազանց ամուր է:

Ayn ch'ap'azants' amur e:

363 - 2

I need to earn money.

Ես պետք է գումար վաստակեմ.

Yes petk' e gumar vastakem.

363 - 3

What time is it?

Ժամը քանիսն է?

Zhamy k'anisn e?

363 - 4

I haven't tried it on.

Ես չեմ փորձել այն:

Yes ch'em p'vordzel ayn:

363 - 5

When will they come?

Ե՞րբ են գալու:

Ye°rb yen galu.

363 - 6

I wish he gets well.

Մաղթում եմ, որ նա առողջանա:

Maght'um yem, vor na arroghjana:

363 - 7

I like old cars.

Ես սիրում եմ հին մեքենաներ:

Yes sirum yem hin mek'enaner:

52/52

Day 363

Test 52

364 - 1

A leaf fluttered down.

364 - 2

Actually, I like her.

364 - 3

It's going to rain.

364 - 4

This bra is too large.

364 - 5

Talk to you later.

364 - 6

It's too tight.

364 - 7

I like old cars.

52/52

Day 364

See you soon

Learn English in 52 weeks
Learn French in 52 weeks
Learn Bulgarian in 52 weeks
Learn Chinese in 52 weeks
Learn Czech in 52 weeks
Learn Danish in 52 weeks
Learn Dutch in 52 weeks
Learn Estonian in 52 weeks
Learn Finnish in 52 weeks
Learn German in 52 weeks
Learn Greek in 52 weeks
Learn Hungarian in 52 weeks
Learn Italian in 52 weeks
Learn Japanese in 52 weeks
Learn Latvian in 52 weeks
Learn Lithuanian in 52 weeks
Learn Polish in 52 weeks
Learn Portuguese in 52 weeks
Learn Brazilian in 52 weeks
Learn Romanian in 52 weeks
Learn Russian in 52 weeks
Learn Slovak in 52 weeks
Learn Spanish in 52 weeks
Learn Swedish in 52 weeks

Made in the USA
Middletown, DE
02 November 2023

41854769R00205